Ben Stacy Jerrik (Ed.)

Scenechronize

Ben Stacy Jerrik (Ed.)

Scenechronize

Computing platform, Information technology, User interface

Part Press

Imprint

Publisher:
Part Press is a trademark of
International Book Market Service Ltd., 17 Rue Meldrum, Beau Bassin, 1713-01 Mauritius
Email: info@bookmarketservice.com
Website: www.bookmarketservice.com

Published in 2012

Printed in: U.S.A., U.K., Germany. This book was not produced in Mauritius.

ISBN: 978-613-6-27453-9

Contents

Articles

References

Scenechronize

scenechronize is a computer software platform, developed by Clever Machine Inc., used mainly by television and movie production companies. Its purpose is to reduce the need for paper materials used during the production process, in order to reduce waste. Clever Machine was founded in December 2003 and incorporated in California. The founders, Hunter Hancock, chief executive officer, and Darren Ehlers, chief operations officer, and five engineers had originally provided customized solutions to financial services companies, assisting in marketing and engineering positions with multiple enterprise software companies. The company's first project was to provide an outsourced information technology team to a financial services company. From there, the company was able to begin its own software company, scenechronize.

Using a Web-based user interface, scenechronize organizes different production aspects — the script, locations, casting, breakdown elements, and schedule. Tools have been specifically created for assistant directors, line producers, above-the-line and below-the-line crews. Each team member has access to his or her own department, while the unit production manager or line producer maintains an overall view, with the option to share that information with other crew members on an as-needed basis. "People can see the project change in real time and always have access to the correct version," says Ehlers.

The company officially began in 2006. In 2008, a preview release of scenechronize was demonstrated to an elite group of art directors and unit production managers. The beta release of scenechronize was announced at the Sundance Film Festival in 2009, with the initial public release announced a year later, also at Sundance. Those selected to test scenechronize appreciated the potential to eliminate communication and collaboration errors.[1] Ehlers noted, "a good example is handling script revisions. During production, if a crew has been shooting for 10 hours and they get a script revision, it can take anywhere from two to six hours to process that. We can reduce that to an hour. When there's a script revision, the program generates a report for each user, showing everything that has changed - every scene and every line, every character -- anything that has changed, we tell you in this report."

scenechronize is now in use at almost every studio and network and with numerous independent films. The company is privately financed, starting with the profits from the outsourcing project described above. The company's engineering offices are in San Francisco, while the sales and support offices are in Burbank, California. All support team members in Burbank have worked with productions ranging from short films and "indies" to network television and studio features.

Companies and productions assisted

Network television

- ABC – No Ordinary Family • FlashForward • Ugly Betty
- AMC – The Walking Dead • Rubicon
- CBS – 90210
- HBO
- DreamWorks Television
- Showtime – United States of Tara • Dexter
- Sony Pictures Television – Breaking Bad
- Valhalla
- Warner Bros. Television

Movie productions

- Bad Robot Productions
- Columbia Pictures – Premium Rush
- Lakeshore Entertainment
- Montecito Picture Company
- Playtone Productions
- Screen Gems
- Skydance Productions
- Spyglass Entertainment
- 20th Century Fox – Water for Elephants • We Bought a Zoo
- Universal Studios – Bridesmaids • Larry Crowne
- Warner Bros. – Due Date

References

[1] Review of Scenechronize Film Production Management Software (http://donschaffer.wordpress.com/2011/03/02/review-of-scenechronize-film-production-management-software/), Schaffer, Don. Wordpress.com, March 2, 2011. Retrieved February 17, 2012.

External links

- scenechronize website (http://www.scenechronize.com/)

Computing_platform

A **computing platform** includes a hardware architecture and a software framework (including application frameworks), where the combination allows software, particularly application software, to run. Typical platforms include a computer's architecture, operating system, programming languages and related user interface (run-time system libraries or graphical user interface).

A platform is a crucial element in software development. A platform might be simply defined as a place to launch software. The platform provider offers the software developer an undertaking that logic code will run consistently as long as the platform is running on top of other platforms. Logic code includes bytecode, source code, and machine code. It actually means execution of the program is not restricted by the type of operating system provided. It has mostly replaced the machine-independent languages.

Some software platforms emulate entire hardware platforms - as in systems virtualization.

Operating-system examples

- AmigaOS, AmigaOS 4
- FreeBSD, NetBSD, OpenBSD
- Linux
- Mac OS X
- Microsoft Windows
- OS/2
- Solaris
- Unix
- IBM VM/370, VM/BSEP, VM/SEP, VM/XA, VM/ESA, z/VM
- Google Chrome OS

Mobile

- Android
- Bada
- BlackBerry OS
- iOS
- Embedded Linux
- Palm OS
- Symbian
- WebOS
- Windows Mobile
- Windows Phone

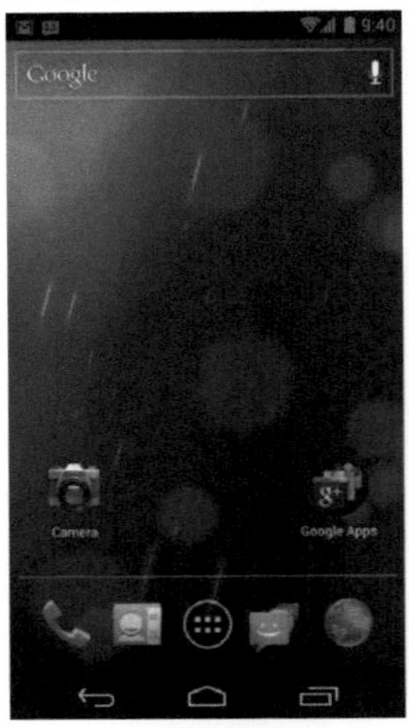

Android, a popular mobile operating system

Software framework examples

- Adobe AIR
- Java, JDK and JRE
- Mono
- Mozilla Prism XUL and XULRunner
- .NET Framework
- Oracle Database
- Vexi

Mobile

- APOXI
- Binary Runtime Environment for Wireless (BREW)
- Java Platform, Micro Edition (Java ME)
- JavaFX Mobile
- Qt
- Smartface Platform

.NET

The umbrella-term .NET applies to a wide set of products and technologies from Microsoft. Most have in common a dependence on the Microsoft .NET Framework, and the Common Language Infrastructure (CLI).

Java

The Java platform runs programs written in the Java language. Java source code is "compiled" to an intermediate-language bytecode which is then interpreted by an interpreter, the Java Virtual Machine (JVM), which then interfaces that program with the Java software libraries. In smartphones, personal digital assistants (PDAs) and other wireless mobile devices, these libraries are the Java ME. Some phones, even without a full operating system, enable Java programs such as games to operate. Java and the bytecode are said to be platform-independent. But this is because Java *is* the platform as well as a programming language. Software really cannot operate without a platform or be platform independent. The programming language is referred to here, meaning the programmer need not be concerned about the hardware or operating system platform, nor will the language change with a different platform.

SAP NetWeaver

SAP NetWeaver is SAP's integrated technology computing platform and is the technical foundation for many SAP applications since the SAP Business Suite. SAP NetWeaver is marketed as a service-oriented application and integration platform. SAP NetWeaver provides the development and runtime environment for SAP applications and can be used for custom development and integration with other applications and systems. SAP NetWeaver is built using primarily the ABAP programming language, but also uses C (programming language), C++, and Java EE. It also employs open standards and industry de facto standards and can be extended with, and interoperate with, technologies such as Microsoft .NET, Java EE, and IBM WebSphere.

Hardware examples

Ordered roughly, from more common types to less common types:

- Commodity computing platforms
  - Wintel, that is, Intel x86 or compatible personal computer hardware with Windows operating system
  - ARM architecture used in mobile devices
    - Gumstix full function miniature computers with Linux
  - x86 with Unix-like systems such as BSD variants
  - CP/M computers based on the S-100 bus, maybe the earliest microcomputer platform
- Video game consoles, any variety
- Macintosh, custom Apple Computer hardware and Mac OS operating system, now migrated to x86
  - Newton devices running the Newton OS, also from Apple
- RISC processor based machines running Unix variants
  - SPARC architecture computers running Solaris operating systems
  - DEC Alpha cluster running OpenVMS
- Midrange computers with their custom operating systems, such as IBM OS/400
- Mainframe computers with their custom operating systems, such as IBM z/OS
- Supercomputer architectures

See also

- Application programming interface
- Compatibility layer
- Just-in-time compilation
- Platform technology

Information_technology

Information Technology (**IT**) is the branch of engineering that deals with the use of computers and telecommunications to store, retrieve and transmit information.[1] The acquisition, processing, storage and dissemination of vocal, pictorial, textual and numerical information by a microelectronics-based combination of computing and telecommunications are its main fields.[2] The term in its modern sense first appeared in a 1958 article published in the *Harvard Business Review*, in which authors Leavitt and Whisler commented that "the new technology does not yet have a single established name. We shall call it information technology (IT)."[3] Some of the modern and emerging fields of Information technology are next generation web technologies, bioinformatics, cloud computing, global information systems, large scale knowledgebases, etc. Advancements are mainly driven in the field of computer science.

Information

The English word was apparently derived from the Latin stem (*information-*) of the nominative (*informatio*): this noun is in its turn derived from the verb "informare" (to inform) in the sense of "to give form to the mind", "to discipline", "instruct", "teach".

Technology

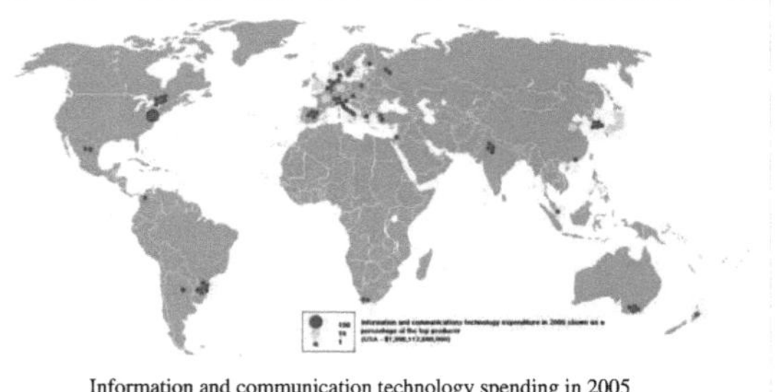
Information and communication technology spending in 2005

IT is the area of managing technology and spans a wide variety of areas that include computer software, information systems, computer hardware, programming languages but are not limited to things such as processes, and data constructs. In short, anything that renders data, information or perceived knowledge in any visual format whatsoever, via any multimedia distribution mechanism, is considered part of the IT domain. IT provides businesses with four sets of core services to help execute the business strategy: business process automation, providing information, connecting with customers, and productivity tools.

IT professionals perform a variety of functions that range from installing applications to designing complex computer networks and information databases. A few of the duties that IT professionals perform may include data management, networking, engineering computer hardware, database and software design, as well as management and administration of entire systems. Information technology is starting to spread further than the conventional personal computer and network technologies, and more into integrations of other technologies such as the use of cell phones, televisions, automobiles, and more, which is increasing the demand for such jobs.

In the recent past, the Accreditation Board for Engineering and Technology and the Association for Computing Machinery have collaborated to form accreditation and curriculum standards[4] for degrees in Information Technology as a distinct field of study as compared[5] to Computer Science and Information Systems today. SIGITE (Special Interest Group for IT Education)[6] is the ACM working group for defining these standards. The Worldwide IT services revenue totaled $763 billion in 2009.[7]

Technological capacity and growth

Hilbert and Lopez[8] identify the exponential pace of technological change (a kind of Moore's law): machines' application-specific capacity to compute information per capita has roughly doubled every 14 months between 1986-2007; the per capita capacity of the world's general-purpose computers has doubled every 18 months during the same two decades; the global telecommunication capacity per capita doubled every 34 months; the world's storage capacity per capita required roughly 40 months to double (every 3 years); and per capita broadcast information has doubled roughly every 12.3 years.[8]

See also

- Information and communications technology (ICT)
- Information history
- Computer science

References

[1] "Princeton WordNet Search 3.1" (http://wordnetweb.princeton.edu/perl/webwn?s=information+technology&sub=Search+WordNet&o2=&o0=1&o8=1&o1=1&o7=&o5=&o9=&o6=&o3=&o4=&h). . Retrieved 2012-04-07.

[2] Longley, Dennis; Shain, Michael (2012), *Dictionary of Information Technology* (2 ed.), Macmillan Press, p. 164, ISBN 0-333-37260-3

[3] Management in the 1980's (http://hbr.org/1958/11/management-in-the-1980s), Harold J. Leavitt and Thomas L. Whisler, Harvard Business Review, 1958-11.

[4] ABET (http://www.abet.org/forms.shtml#For_Computing_Programs_Only)

[5] Isbell, Charles; Impagliazzo, John; Stein, Lynn; Proulx, Viera; Russ, Steve; Forbes, Jeffrey; Thomas, Richard; Fraser, Linda et al. (December 2009), *(Re)Defining Computing Curricula by (Re)Defining Computing*, Association for Computing Machinery, ACM, ISBN 978-1-60558-886-5

[6] ACM-SIGITE (http://www.sigite.org/)

[7] "Gartner Says Worldwide IT Services Revenue Declined 5.3 Percent in 2009" (http://www.gartner.com/it/page.jsp?id=1363713), Gartner, , retrieved 20 November 2010

[8] "The World's Technological Capacity to Store, Communicate, and Compute Information" (http://www.sciencemag.org/content/332/6025/60), Martin Hilbert and Priscila López (2011), Science (journal), 332(6025), 60-65; free access to the article through here: martinhilbert.net/WorldInfoCapacity.html

Further reading

- Adelman, C. (2000). *A Parallel Post-secondary Universe: The Certification System in Information Technology*. Washington, D.C.: U.S. Department of Education.
- Allen, T., and M.S. Morton, eds. 1994. *Information Technology and the Corporation of the 1990s*. New York: Oxford University Press.
- Shelly, Gary, Cashman, Thomas, Vermaat, Misty, and Walker, Tim. (1999). *Discovering Computers 2000: Concepts for a Connected World*. Cambridge, Massachusetts: Course Technology.
- Webster, Frank, and Robins, Kevin. (1986). *Information Technology—A Luddite Analysis*. Norwood, NJ: Ablex.
- *The Global Information Technology Report 2008–2009* (http://www.weforum.org/pdf/gitr/2009/gitr09fullreport.pdf), World Economic Forum and INSEAD, 2009, ISBN 978-92-95044-19-7
- Blais, Steven (December 2011). *Business Analysis: Best Practices for Success*. John Wiley & Sons. ISBN 1118076001.

External links

- The Information Technology Infrastructure Library (ITIL) (http://www.itil-officialsite.com/home/home.asp)

User_interface

The **user interface**, in the industrial design field of human–machine interaction, is the space where interaction between humans and machines occurs. The goal of interaction between a human and a machine at the user interface is effective operation and control of the machine, and feedback from the machine which aids the operator in making operational decisions. Examples of this broad concept of user interfaces include the interactive aspects of computer operating systems, hand tools, heavy machinery operator controls, and process controls. The design considerations applicable when creating user interfaces are related to or involve such disciplines as ergonomics and psychology.

A user interface is the system by which people (users) interact with a machine. The user interface includes hardware (physical) and software (logical) components. User interfaces exist for various systems, and provide a means of:

- Input, allowing the users to manipulate a system
- Output, allowing the system to indicate the effects of the users' manipulation

Generally, the goal of human-machine interaction engineering is to produce a user interface which makes it easy, efficient, and enjoyable to operate a machine in the way which produces the desired result. This generally means that the operator needs to provide minimal input to achieve the desired output, and also that the machine minimizes undesired outputs to the human.

Ever since the increased use of personal computers and the relative decline in societal awareness of heavy machinery, the term user interface has taken on overtones of the graphical user interface, while industrial control panel and machinery control design discussions more commonly refer to human-machine interfaces.

Other terms for user interface include **human–computer interface** (**HCI**) and **man–machine interface** (**MMI**).

Introduction

To work with a system, users have to be able to control and assess the state of the system. For example, when driving an automobile, the driver uses the steering wheel to control the direction of the vehicle, and the accelerator pedal, brake pedal and gearstick to control the speed of the vehicle. The driver perceives the position of the vehicle by looking through the windshield and exact speed of the vehicle by reading the speedometer. The *user interface of the automobile* is on the whole composed of the instruments the driver can use to accomplish the tasks of driving and maintaining the automobile.

Terminology

There is a difference between a user interface and an operator interface or a human–machine interface.

- The term "user interface" is often used in the context of (personal) computer systems and electronic devices
  - Where a network of equipment or computers are interlinked through an MES (Manufacturing Execution System)-or Host.
  - An HMI is typically local to one machine or piece of equipment, and is the interface method between the human and the equipment/machine. An Operator interface is the interface method by which multiple equipment that are linked by a host control system is accessed or controlled.
  - The system may expose several user interfaces to serve different kinds of users. For example, a computerized library database might provide two user interfaces, one for library patrons (limited set of functions, optimized for ease of use) and the other for library personnel (wide set of functions, optimized for efficiency).

- The user interface of a mechanical system, a vehicle or an industrial installation is sometimes referred to as the human–machine interface (HMI). HMI is a modification of the original term MMI (man-machine interface). In practice, the abbreviation MMI is still frequently used although some may claim that MMI stands for something different now. Another abbreviation is HCI, but is more commonly used for human-computer interaction. Other terms used are operator interface console (OIC) and operator interface terminal (OIT). However it is abbreviated, the terms refer to the 'layer' that separates a human that is operating a machine from the machine itself.

HMI of a machine for the sugar industry with pushbuttons

In science fiction, HMI is sometimes used to refer to what is better described as direct neural interface. However, this latter usage is seeing increasing application in the real-life use of (medical) prostheses—the artificial extension that replaces a missing body part (e.g., cochlear implants).

In some circumstance computers might observe the user, and react according to their actions without specific commands. A means of tracking parts of the body is required, and sensors noting the position of the head, direction of gaze and so on have been used experimentally. This is particularly relevant to immersive interfaces.

Usability

See also: mental model, human action cycle, usability testing, and ergonomics. List of human-computer interaction topics

User interfaces are considered by some authors to be a prime ingredient of Computer user satisfaction.

The design of a user interface affects the amount of effort the user must expend to provide input for the system and to interpret the output of the system, and how much effort it takes to learn how to do this. Usability is the degree to which the design of a particular user interface takes into account the human psychology and physiology of the users, and makes the process of using the system effective, efficient and satisfying.

Usability is mainly a characteristic of the user interface, but is also associated with the functionalities of the product and the process to design it. It describes how well a product can be used for its intended purpose by its target users with efficiency, effectiveness, and satisfaction, also taking into account the requirements from its context of use.

User interfaces in computing

In computer science and human-computer interaction, the *user interface (of a computer program)* refers to the graphical, textual and auditory information the program presents to the user, and the control sequences (such as keystrokes with the computer keyboard, movements of the computer mouse, and selections with the touchscreen) the user employs to control the program.

Types

Direct manipulation interface is the name of a general class of user interfaces that allow users to manipulate objects presented to them, using actions that correspond at least loosely to the physical world.

Currently (as of 2009) the following types of user interface are the most common:

- **Graphical user interfaces** (GUI) accept input via devices such as computer keyboard and mouse and provide articulated graphical output on the computer monitor. There are at least two different principles widely used in GUI design: Object-oriented user interfaces (OOUIs) and application oriented interfaces.

- **Web-based user interfaces** or **web user interfaces** (WUI) are a subclass of GUIs that accept input and provide output by generating web pages which are transmitted via the Internet and viewed by the user using a web browser program. Newer implementations utilize Java, AJAX, Adobe Flex, Microsoft .NET, or similar technologies to provide real-time control in a separate program, eliminating the need to refresh a traditional HTML based web browser. Administrative web interfaces for web-servers, servers and networked computers are often called control panels.
- **Touchscreens** are displays that accept input by touch of fingers or a stylus. Used in a growing amount of mobile devices and many types of point of sale, industrial processes and machines, self-service machines etc.

User interfaces that are common in various fields outside desktop computing:

- **Command line interfaces**, where the user provides the input by typing a command string with the computer keyboard and the system provides output by printing text on the computer monitor. Used by programmers and system administrators, in engineering and scientific environments, and by technically advanced personal computer users.
- **Touch user interface** are graphical user interfaces using a touchpad or touchscreen display as a combined input and output device. They supplement or replace other forms of output with haptic feedback methods. Used in computerized simulators etc.

Other types of user interfaces:

- **Attentive user interfaces** manage the user attention deciding when to interrupt the user, the kind of warnings, and the level of detail of the messages presented to the user.
- **Batch interfaces** are non-interactive user interfaces, where the user specifies all the details of the *batch job* in advance to batch processing, and receives the output when all the processing is done. The computer does not prompt for further input after the processing has started.
- **Conversational Interface Agents** attempt to personify the computer interface in the form of an animated person, robot, or other character (such as Microsoft's Clippy the paperclip), and present interactions in a conversational form.
- **Crossing-based interfaces** are graphical user interfaces in which the primary task consists in crossing boundaries instead of pointing.
- **Gesture interfaces** are graphical user interfaces which accept input in a form of hand gestures, or mouse gestures sketched with a computer mouse or a stylus.
- **Intelligent user interfaces** are human-machine interfaces that aim to improve the efficiency, effectiveness, and naturalness of human-machine interaction by representing, reasoning, and acting on models of the user, domain, task, discourse, and media (e.g., graphics, natural language, gesture).
- **Motion tracking interfaces** monitor the user's body motions and translate them into commands, currently being developed by Apple[1]
- **Multi-screen interfaces**, employ multiple displays to provide a more flexible interaction. This is often employed in computer game interaction in both the commercial arcades and more recently the handheld markets.
- **Noncommand user interfaces**, which observe the user to infer his / her needs and intentions, without requiring that he / she formulate explicit commands.
- **Object-oriented user interfaces (OOUI)** are based on object-oriented programming metaphors, allowing users to manipulate simulated objects and their properties.
- **Reflexive user interfaces** where the users control and redefine the entire system via the user interface alone, for instance to change its command verbs. Typically this is only possible with very rich graphic user interfaces.
- **Tangible user interfaces**, which place a greater emphasis on touch and physical environment or its element.
- **Task-Focused Interfaces** are user interfaces which address the information overload problem of the desktop metaphor by making tasks, not files, the primary unit of interaction

- **Text user interfaces** are user interfaces which output text, but accept other form of input in addition to or in place of typed command strings.
- **Voice user interfaces**, which accept input and provide output by generating voice prompts. The user input is made by pressing keys or buttons, or responding verbally to the interface.
- **Natural-Language interfaces** - Used for search engines and on webpages. User types in a question and waits for a response.
- **Zero-Input interfaces** get inputs from a set of sensors instead of querying the user with input dialogs.
- **Zooming user interfaces** are graphical user interfaces in which information objects are represented at different levels of scale and detail, and where the user can change the scale of the viewed area in order to show more detail.

See also:

- Archy, an experimental keyboard-driven modeless user interface by Jef Raskin, arguably more efficient than mouse-driven user interfaces for document editing and programming.

History

The history of user interfaces can be divided into the following phases according to the dominant type of user interface:

- Batch interface, 1945–1968
- Command-line user interface, 1969 to present
- Graphical user interface, 1981 to present — see History of the GUI for a detailed look

Consistency

A property of a good user interface is consistency. Good user interface design is about getting a user to have a consistent set of expectations, and then meeting those expectations. Consistency can be bad if not used for a purpose and when it serves no benefit for the end user, though; like any other principle, consistency has its limits.[2]

Consistency is one quality to trade off in user interface design as described by the cognitive dimensions framework. In some cases, a violation of consistency principles can provide sufficiently clear advantages that a wise and careful user interface designer may choose to violate consistency to achieve some other important goal.[3]

There are three aspects identified as relevant to consistency.[4]

First, the controls for different features should be presented in a consistent manner so that users can find the controls easily. For example, users find it difficult to use software when some commands are available through menus, some through icons, some through right-clicks, some under a separate button at one corner of a screen, some grouped by function, some grouped by “common,” some grouped by “advanced.” A user looking for a command should have a consistent search strategy for finding it. The more search strategies a user has to use, the more frustrating the search will be. The more consistent the grouping, the easier the search. The principle of monotony of design in user interfaces states that ideally there should be only way to achieve a simple operation,[5] to facilitate habituation to the interface.

Second, there is the "principle of least astonishment". Various features should work in similar ways.[6] For example, some features in Adobe Acrobat are "select tool, then select text to which apply." Others are "select text, then apply action to selection."[7] Commands should work the same way in all contexts.

Third, consistency counsels against user interface changes version-to-version. Change should be minimized, and forward-compatibility should be maintained. Generally, less mature software has fewer users who are entrenched in the status quo. Older, more broadly used software must more carefully hew to the status quo to avoid disruptive costs. For example, the change from the menu bars of Microsoft Office 2003 to the ribbon toolbar of Microsoft Office 2007 caused mixed reactions. The new interface caused rejection among advanced users,[8] who reported losses in productivity,[9] while average users reported improved productivity [8] and a fairly good acceptance.[10] A usual solution in providing a new user interface is to provide a backwards-compatibility mode, so that a product's most intensive users are not forced to bear the costs of the change. A second strategy is to introduce big changes in small increments, so that an overall redesign can be achieved without breaking consistency and providing user feedback at any single step.[11]

Modalities and modes

Two words are used in UI design to describe different ways in which a user can utilize a product. *Modality* refers to several alternate interfaces to the same product, while *mode* describes different states of the same interface.

A modality is a path of communication employed by the user interface to carry input and output. Examples of modalities:

- Input — computer keyboard allows the user to enter typed text, digitizing tablet allows the user to create free-form drawing
- Output — computer monitor allows the system to display text and graphics (*vision modality*), loudspeaker allows the system to produce sound (*auditory modality*)

The user interface may employ several redundant input modalities and output modalities, allowing the user to choose which ones to use for interaction.

A mode is a distinct method of operation within a computer program, in which the same input can produce different perceived results depending of the state of the computer program. For example, caps lock sets an input mode in which typed letters are uppercase by default; the same typing produces lowercase letters when not in caps lock mode. Heavy use of modes often reduces the usability of a user interface, as the user must expend effort to remember current mode states, and switch between mode states as necessary.

See also

- Accessibility and computer accessibility — user interface's suitability for people with special needs
- Adaptive user interfaces
- Brain-computer interface
- Computer user satisfaction
- Distinguishable interfaces
- Ergonomics and human factors — the study of designing objects to be better adapted to the shape of the human body
- Framebuffer
- Graphical User Interface
- Human-computer interaction links
- Icon design
- Information architecture — organizing, naming, and labelling information strctures
- Information visualization — the use of sensory representations of abstract data to reinforce cognition
- Interaction design
- Interaction technique
- Interface (computer science)
- Kinetic user interface
- Knowledge visualization — the use of visual representations to transfer knowledge
- List of user interface literature
- Natural user interfaces
- Ncurses, a semigraphical user interface.
- Organic user interface
- Post-WIMP

- Tangible user interface
- Unified Code for Units of Measure
- Usability links
- User Assistance
- User experience
- User experience design
- User interface design
- Virtual artifact
- Virtual user interface

References

[1] appleinsider.com (http://www.appleinsider.com/articles/09/06/18/apple_exploring_motion_tracking_mac_os_x_user_interface.html)

[2] "How to avoid foolish consistency" (http://www.scottberkun.com/essays/5-how-to-avoid-foolish-consistency). . "People don't like to learn things. If they take the time to learn something, they expect to be able to apply that knowledge in many places. It follows that good designers conserve the number of things users need to learn to get stuff done. ... In rare cases, consistency can become a self-perpetuating monster: It has to be used for a purpose. A foolish consistency is one that serves no benefit for the end user. Making things look and work the same is pointless if the user can no longer accomplish their tasks. Rank making things useful above making them consistent. ... Consistency is great because people like predictable things. They will feel comfortable when they can rely on different parts of your product to do exactly what they think it will do."

[3] T. R. G. Green and M. Petre. Usability analysis of visual programming environments: A `cognitive dimensions' framework. Journal of Visual Languages and Computing, 7:131—174, 1996. (http://citeseerx.ist.psu.edu/viewdoc/summary?doi=10.1.1.22.1477)

[4] David E. Boundy (October 1991). "A taxonomy of programmers" (http://alcor.concordia.ca/~smw/home/resources/taxonomy.html). *ACM SIGSOFT Software Engineering Notes 16(4) 23-30*. alcor.concordia.ca. .

[5] Summary of design rules from *The Humane Interface* (http://Nitpicker.PBwiki.com/The+Humane+Interface)

[6] For example, inconsistent user interface was one of the major causes of the Three Mile Island nuclear accident in 1979. Some indicator lights indicated normal as red, some as green. iem-inc.com (http://www.iem-inc.com/TMI.pdf)

[7] help.adobe.com (http://help.adobe.com/en_US/Acrobat/8.0/Professional/gs.pdf)

[8] Word 2007: Not Exactly a Must-Have (http://redmondmag.com/features/article.asp?editorialsid=2346)

[9] "Ribbon survey results" (http://www.exceluser.com/explore/surveys/ribbon/ribbon-survey-results.htm). .

[10] "Dostál, M. User Acceptance of the Microsoft Ribbon User Interface" (http://www.wseas.us/e-library/conferences/2010/Faro/DNCOCO/DNCOCO-25.pdf). ., In: *Advances in data networks, communications, computers*. pp 143-149, WSEAS Press, 2010. ISBN 978-960-474-245-5

[11] Jeffrey Veen. "Case Study: Intranets, Usability, and Value" (http://veen.com/jeff/archives/000653.html). . "All too often an intranet redesign fails because users don't adopt the new mechanisms for creating and distributing content — this can be mitigated by choosing early projects that focus on commonly recognized quick wins. Her plan should have a long-term vision, but it should be implemented in small increments that instill a sense of confidence and value among users throughout the redesign. Small increments allow for course corrections toward the long-term vision."

External links

- Its bibliography (http://www.interaction-design.org/references/conferences/) covers a wide area of user interface publications
- Chapter 2. History: A brief History of user interfaces (http://www.catb.org/~esr/writings/taouu/html/ch02.html)

Software_release_life_cycle

A **software release life cycle** refers to the phases of development and maturity for a piece of computer software—ranging from its initial development, to its eventual release, and updated versions of the released version to help improve software or fix bugs still present in the software.

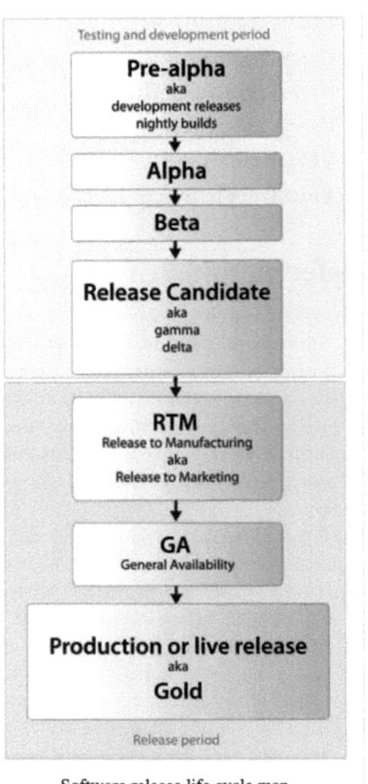

Software release life cycle map

Stages of development

Pre-alpha

Pre-alpha refers to all activities performed during the software project prior to testing. These activities can include requirements analysis, software design, software development, and unit testing.

In typical open source development, there are several types of pre-alpha versions. **Milestone** versions include specific sets of functions and are released as soon as the functionality is complete.

Alpha

The alpha phase of the release life cycle is the first phase to begin software testing (alpha is the first letter of the Greek alphabet, used as the number 1). In this phase, developers generally test the software using white box techniques. Additional validation is then performed using black box or gray box techniques, by another testing team. Moving to black box testing inside the organization is known as *alpha release*.[1]

Alpha software can be unstable and could cause crashes or data loss. The exception to this is when the alpha is available publicly (such as a pre-order bonus), in which developers normally push for stability so that their testers can test properly. External availability of alpha software is uncommon in proprietary software. However, open source software, in particular, often have publicly available alpha versions, often distributed as the raw source code of the software.

The alpha phase usually ends with a feature freeze, indicating that no more features will be added to the software. At this time, the software is said to be a feature complete.

Beta

Beta (named after the second letter of the Greek alphabet) is the software development phase following alpha. It generally begins when the software is feature complete. Software in the beta phase will generally have many more bugs in it than completed software, as well as speed/performance issues. The focus of beta testing is reducing impacts to users, often incorporating usability testing. The process of delivering a beta version to the users is called **beta release** and this is typically the first time that the software is available outside of the organization that developed it.

The users of a beta version are called *beta testers*. They are usually customers or prospective customers of the organization that develops the software, willing to test the software without charge, often receiving the final software free of charge or for a reduced price.

Beta version software is often useful for demonstrations and previews within an organization and to prospective customers. Some developers refer to this stage as a **preview**, **prototype**, **technical preview** (**TP**), or **early access**.

Some software is kept in perpetual beta—where new features and functionality are continually added to the software without establishing a firm "final" release.

Open and closed beta

Developers release either a **closed beta** or an **open beta**; closed beta versions are released to a restricted group of individuals for a user test by invitation, while open beta testers are from a larger group, or anyone interested. The testers report any bugs that they find, and sometimes suggest additional features they think should be available in the final version. Examples of a major public beta test are:

- In September 2000 a *boxed version* of Apple's Mac OS X Public Beta operating system was released.[2]
- Microsoft's release of **community technology previews** (**CTPs**) for "Longhorn" in January 2005.[3]

Open betas serve the dual purpose of demonstrating a product to potential consumers, and testing among an extremely wide user base likely to bring to light obscure errors that a much smaller testing team may not find.

Release candidate

A **release candidate** (**RC**) is a beta version with potential to be a final product, which is ready to release unless significant bugs emerge. In this stage of product stabilization, all product features have been designed, coded and tested through one or more beta cycles with no known showstopper-class bug.

A release is called **code complete** when the development team agrees that no entirely new source code will be added to this release. There may still be source code changes to fix defects, and changes to documentation and data files, and to the code for test cases or utilities.

Release

RTM

The term "**release to manufacturing**" or "**release to marketing**" (both abbreviated RTM, initials also commonly used for the quite different "return to manufacturer" of faulty goods)—also known as "going gold"—is a term used when software is ready for or has been delivered or provided to the customer. It is typically used in certain retail mass-production software contexts—as opposed to a specialized software production or project in a commercial or government production and distribution—where the software is sold as part of a bundle in a related computer hardware sale and typically where the software and related hardware is ultimately to be available and sold on mass/public basis at retail stores to indicate that the software has met a defined quality level and is ready for mass retail distribution. RTM could also mean in other contexts that the software has been delivered or released to a client or customer for installation or distribution to the related hardware end user computers or machines. The term does *not* define the delivery mechanism or volume; it only states that the quality is sufficient for mass distribution. The deliverable from the engineering organization is frequently in the form of a **gold** master CD used for duplication or to produce the image for the web.

RTM precedes general availability (GA) when the product is released to the public.

General availability (GA)

General availability or **general acceptance** (**GA**) is the point where all necessary commercialization activities have been completed and the software has been made available to the general market either via the web or physical media. Another term with a meaning almost identical to GA is **first customer shipment** (**FCS**). Some companies (such as Sun Microsystems and Cisco) use FCS to describe a software version that has been shipped for revenue.

Commercialization activities could include but are not limited to the availability of media world wide via dispersed distribution centers, marketing collateral is completed and available in as many languages as deemed necessary for the target market, the finishing of security and compliance tests, etc. The time between RTM and GA can be from a week to months in some cases before a generally available release can be declared because of the time needed to complete all commercialization activities required by GA.

It is also at this stage that the software is considered to have "gone live". The **production**, **live** version is the final version of a particular product. A live release is considered to be very stable and relatively bug-free with a quality suitable for wide distribution and use by end users. In commercial software releases, this version may also be signed (used to allow end-users to verify that code has not been modified since the release). The expression that a software product "has gone live" means that the code has been completed and is ready for distribution. Other terms for the live version include *live master*, *live release*, and *live build*.

In some areas of software development it is at this stage that the release is referred to as a **grand** or **gold** release; the latter seems to be confined mainly to game software though Apple also refer to GM (gold master) releases.

Some release versions might be classified as a long term support (LTS) release, which should guarantee the ability to upgrade to the next LTS release and will be supported/updated/patched for a longer time than a non-LTS release.

Support

During its supported lifetime, software is sometimes subjected to service releases, or service packs, sometimes also called "interim releases". For example, Microsoft's Windows XP operating system had three major service packs during its lifetime.

Such service releases contain a collection of updates, fixes and enhancements, delivered in the form of a single installable package. They may also implement new features.

Some software is released with the expectation of regular support. Classes of software that generally involve protracted support as the norm include anti-virus suites and massively multiplayer online games.

End-of-life

When software is no longer sold or supported, the product is said to have reached end-of-life, to be discontinued or obsolete, but user loyalty may continue its existence for some time, even long after its platform is obsolete—e.g., the Atari ST and Commodore's Amiga.

Impact of the World Wide Web

As the Internet has facilitated rapid and inexpensive distribution of software, companies have begun to take a looser approach to use of the word "beta".[4] Netscape Communications was infamous for releasing alpha level versions of its Netscape web browser to the public and calling them "beta" releases. In February 2005 ZDNet published an article about the recent phenomenon of a beta version often staying for years and being used as if it were in production level, disparagingly called "perpetual beta". It noted that Gmail and Google News, for example, had been in beta for a long period of time and were not expected to drop the beta status despite the fact that they were widely used; however, Google News did leave beta in January 2006, followed by Google Apps, including Gmail, in July 2009.[5] This technique may allow a developer to delay offering full support and responsibility for remaining issues.

In the context of Web 2.0, people even talk of perpetual betas to signify that some software is meant to stay in beta state. Also, "beta" is sometimes used to indicate something more like a release candidate, or as a form of time limited demo, or marketing technique.[6]

Some users disparagingly refer to release candidates and even final "point oh" releases as "gamma test" software, suggesting that the developer has chosen to use its customers to test software that is not truly ready for general release. Beta testers, if privately selected, will often be credited for using the release candidate as though it were a finished product.

Web release

A **web release** is a means of software delivery that utilizes the Internet for distribution. No physical media are produced in this type of release mechanism by the manufacturer. This is sometimes also referred to as *release to web* (RTW). Web releases became more common as Internet usage grew.

See also

- Paper launch
- Release engineering
- Release management
- Rolling release
- Software maintenance
- Software testing
- Software versioning
- Software deployment
- Vaporware

References

[1] "Encyclopedia definition of alpha version" (http://www.pcmag.com/encyclopedia_term/0,2542,t=alpha+version&i=37675,00.asp). *PC Magazine*. . Retrieved 12 January 2011.

[2] "Apple Releases Mac OS X Public Beta" (http://www.apple.com/pr/library/2000/sep/13macosx.html) (Press release). Apple Inc.. 13 September 2000. . Retrieved 22 February 2011.

[3] "Microsoft Windows Vista October Community Technology Preview Fact Sheet" (http://www.microsoft.com/presspass/newsroom/winxp/WinVistaCTPFS.mspx) (Press release). Microsoft. October 2005. . Retrieved 22 February 2011.

[4] "Waiting with Beta'd Breath *TidBITS* #328 (May 13, 1996)" (http://web.archive.org/web/20060515093203/http://www.tidbits.com/tb-issues/TidBITS-328.html). Archived from the original (http://www.tidbits.com/tb-issues/TidBITS-328.html) on 2006-05-15. .

[5] "Google Apps is out of beta (yes, really)" (http://googleblog.blogspot.com/2009/07/google-apps-is-out-of-beta-yes-really.html). *Google Blog*. Google. 7 July 2009. . Retrieved 12 January 2011.

[6] The inconvenient truths behind betas (http://www.gamesradar.com/f/the-inconvenient-truths-behind-betas/a-2010051712402686048)

Further reading

- *Continuous Delivery: Reliable Software Releases through Build, Test, and Deployment Automation* by Jez Humble, David Farley; ISBN 0-321-60191-2

External links

- Free Software Project Management HOWTO (http://www.tldp.org/HOWTO/Software-Proj-Mgmt-HOWTO/users.html#ALPHABETA)
- Software Release Decisions (http://www.se-cure.ch/Publications.html)
- A Methodology to Support Software Release Decisions (http://www.methodsandtools.com/archive/archive.php?id=55)
- Software Testing Life Cycle (http://www.editorial.co.in/software/software-testing-life-cycle.php)
- Semantic versioning (http://semver.org/)

Independent_film

An **Independent film** is a professional film production resulting in a feature film that is produced mostly or completely outside of the major film studio system. In addition to being produced and distributed by independent entertainment companies, independent films are also produced and/or distributed by subsidiaries of major film studios. Independent films are sometimes distinguishable by their content and style and the way in which the filmmakers' personal artistic vision is realized. Usually, but not always, independent films are made with considerably lower film budgets than major studio films.[1] Generally, the marketing of independent films is characterized by limited release, but can also have major marketing campaigns and a wide release. Independent films are often screened at local, national, or international film festivals before distribution (theatrical and/or retail release). An independent film production can rival a mainstream film production if it has the necessary funding and distribution.

History

Resistance to the Edison Trust

The roots of independent film can be traced back to the filmmakers in the 1900s who resisted the control of a trust called the Motion Picture Patents Company or "Edison Trust." The Motion Picture Patents Company, founded in December 1908, was a trust of all the major film companies (Edison, Biograph, Vitagraph, Essanay, Selig, Lubin, Kalem, American Star, American Pathé), the leading distributor (George Kleine) and the biggest supplier of raw film, Eastman Kodak.

At the time of the formation of the MPPC, Thomas Edison owned most of the major patents relating to motion pictures, including that for raw film. The MPPC vigorously enforced its patents, constantly bringing suits and receiving injunctions against independent filmmakers. Because of this, a number of filmmakers responded by building their own cameras and moving their operations to Hollywood, California, where the distance from Edison's home base of New Jersey made it more difficult for the MPPC to enforce its patents.[2]

The Edison Trust was soon ended by two decisions of the Supreme Court of the United States: one in 1912, which canceled the patent on raw film, and a second in 1915, which cancelled all MPPC patents. Though these decisions succeeded at legalizing independent film, they would do little to remedy the de facto ban on small productions; the independent filmmakers who had fled to Southern California during the enforcement of the trust had already laid the groundwork for the studio system of classical Hollywood cinema.

The studio system replaces Edison

In early 1910, director D.W. Griffith was sent by the Biograph Company to the west coast with his acting troupe, consisting of actors Blanche Sweet, Lillian Gish, Mary Pickford, Lionel Barrymore, and others. They started filming on a vacant lot near Georgia Street in downtown Los Angeles. While there, the company decided to explore new territories, traveling several miles north to Hollywood, a little village that was friendly and enjoyed the movie company filming there. Griffith then filmed the first movie ever shot in Hollywood, *In Old California*, a Biograph melodrama about California in the 1800s, while it belonged to Mexico. Biograph stayed there for months and made several films before returning to New York.

During the Edison era of the early 1900s, many Jewish immigrants had found employment in the U.S. film industry. Under the Edison Trust, they were able to make their mark in a brand-new business: the exhibition of films in storefront theaters called nickelodeons. Within a few years, ambitious men like Samuel Goldwyn, Carl Laemmle, Adolph Zukor, Louis B. Mayer, and the Warner Brothers (Harry, Albert, Samuel, and Jack) had switched to the production side of the business. After hearing about Biograph's success in Hollywood, in 1913 many such would-be movie-makers headed west to avoid the fees imposed by Edison. Soon they were the heads of a new kind of enterprise: the movie studio.

By establishing a new system of production, distribution, and exhibition which was independent of The Edison Trust in New York, these studios opened up new horizons for cinema in the United States. The Hollywood oligopoly replaced the Edison monopoly. Within this new system, a pecking order was soon established which left little room for any newcomers. At the top were the five major studios, 20th Century Fox, Metro-Goldwyn-Mayer, Paramount Pictures, RKO Pictures, and Warner Bros. Beneath them were Columbia Pictures, United Artists, and Universal Studios. Finally there was "Poverty Row," a catch all term used to encompass any other smaller studio that managed to fight their way up into the increasingly exclusive movie business. It is worth noting that though the small studios that made up Poverty Row could be characterized as existing "independently" of any major studio, they utilized the same kind of vertically and horizontally integrated systems of business as the larger players in the game. Though the eventual breakup of the studio system and its restrictive chain-theater distribution network would leave independent movie houses eager for the kind of populist, seat-filling product of the Poverty Row studios, that same paradigm shift would also lead to the decline and ultimate disappearance of "Poverty Row" as a Hollywood phenomenon. While the kinds of films produced by Poverty Row studios only grew in popularity, they would eventually become increasingly available both from major production companies and from independent producers who no longer needed to rely on a studio's ability to package and release their work.

The following table illustrates the categories commonly used to characterize the Hollywood system.

The Big Five majors	The Little Three majors	Poverty Row (top four of many)
Metro-Goldwyn-Mayer	United Artists	Grand National
Paramount Pictures	Columbia Pictures	Republic Pictures
20th Century Fox	Universal Studios	Monogram Pictures
Warner Bros.		Producers Releasing Corporation (aka PRC)
RKO Pictures		

United Artists and the resistance to the studio system

The studio system quickly became so powerful that some filmmakers once again sought independence as a result. On February 5, 1919 four of the leading figures in American silent cinema (Mary Pickford, Charles Chaplin, Douglas Fairbanks, and D. W. Griffith) formed United Artists, the first independent studio in America. Each held a 20% stake, with the remaining 20% held by lawyer William Gibbs McAdoo.[3] The idea for the venture originated with Fairbanks, Chaplin, Pickford, and cowboy star William S. Hart a year earlier as they were traveling around the U.S.

selling Liberty bonds to help the World War I effort. Already veterans of Hollywood, the four film stars began to talk of forming their own company to better control their own work as well as their futures. They were spurred on by the actions of established Hollywood producers and distributors, who were making moves to tighten their control over their stars' salaries and creative license. With the addition of Griffith, planning began, but Hart bowed out before things had formalized. When he heard about their scheme, Richard A. Rowland, head of Metro Pictures, is said to have observed, "The inmates are taking over the asylum."

The four partners, with advice from McAdoo (son-in-law and former Treasury Secretary of then-President Woodrow Wilson), formed their distribution company, with Hiram Abrams as its first managing director. The original terms called for Pickford, Fairbanks, Griffith and Chaplin to independently produce five pictures each year, but by the time the company got under way in 1920-1921, feature films were becoming more expensive and more polished, and running times had settled at around ninety minutes (or eight reels). It was believed that no one, no matter how popular, could produce and star in five quality feature films a year. By 1924, Griffith had dropped out and the company was facing a crisis: either bring in others to help support a costly distribution system or concede defeat. The veteran producer Joseph Schenck was hired as president. Not only had he been producing pictures for a decade, but he brought along commitments for films starring his wife, Norma Talmadge, his sister-in-law, Constance Talmadge, and his brother-in-law, Buster Keaton. Contracts were signed with a letter of independent producers, especially Samuel Goldwyn, Alexander Korda and Howard Hughes. Schenck also formed a separate partnership with Pickford and Chaplin to buy and build theaters under the United Artists name.

Still, even with a broadening of the company, UA struggled. The coming of sound ended the careers of Pickford and Fairbanks. Chaplin, rich enough to do what he pleased, worked only occasionally. Schenck resigned in 1933 to organize a new company with Darryl F. Zanuck, Twentieth Century Pictures, which soon provided four pictures a year to UA's schedule. He was replaced as president by sales manager Al Lichtman who himself resigned after only a few months. Pickford produced a few films, and at various times Goldwyn, Korda, Walt Disney, Walter Wanger, and David O. Selznick were made "producing partners" (i.e., sharing in the profits), but ownership still rested with the founders. As the years passed and the dynamics of the business changed, these "producing partners" drifted away. Goldwyn and Disney left for RKO, Wanger for Universal Pictures, and Selznick for retirement. By the late 1940s, United Artists had virtually ceased to exist as either a producer or distributor.

The Society of Independent Motion Picture Producers

In 1941, Mary Pickford, Charlie Chaplin, Walt Disney, Orson Welles, Samuel Goldwyn, David O. Selznick, Alexander Korda, and Walter Wanger—many of the same people who were members of United Artists—founded the Society of Independent Motion Picture Producers. Later members included William Cagney, Sol Lesser, and Hal Roach. The Society aimed to preserve the rights of independent producers in an industry overwhelmingly controlled by the studio system. SIMPP fought to end monopolistic practices by the five major Hollywood studios which controlled the production, distribution, and exhibition of films.

In 1942, the SIMPP filed an antitrust suit against Paramount's United Detroit Theatres. The complaint accused Paramount of conspiracy to control first-run and subsequent-run theaters in Detroit. It was the first antitrust suit brought by producers against exhibitors alleging monopoly and restraint of trade.

In 1948, the United States Supreme Court Paramount Decision ordered the Hollywood movie studios to sell their theater chains and to eliminate certain anti-competitive practices. This effectively brought an end to the studio system of Hollywood's Golden Age.

By 1958, many of the reasons for creating the SIMPP had been corrected and SIMPP closed its offices.

Low-budget films

The efforts of the SIMPP and the advent of inexpensive portable cameras during World War II effectively made it possible for any person in America with an interest in making films to write, produce, and direct one without the aide of any major film studio. These circumstances soon resulted in a number of critically acclaimed and highly influential works, including Maya Deren's *Meshes of the Afternoon* in 1943, Kenneth Anger's *Fireworks* in 1947, and Morris Engel, Ruth Orkin and Ray Abrashkin's *Little Fugitive* in 1953. Filmmakers such as Ken Jacobs with little or no formal training began to experiment with new ways of making and shooting films.

Little Fugitive became the first independent film to be nominated for Academy Award for Best Original Screenplay at the American Academy Awards. It also received Silver Lion at Venice. Both Engel and Anger's films won acclaim overseas from the burgeoning French New Wave, with *Fireworks* inspiring praise and an invitation to study under him in Europe from Jean Cocteau, and François Truffaut citing *Little Fugitive* as an essential inspiration to his seminal work, *The 400 Blows*. As the 1950s progressed, the new low-budget paradigm of filmmaking gained increased recognition internationally, with films such Satyajit Ray's critically acclaimed[4] [5] [6] [7] *Apu Trilogy* (1955–1959).

Unlike films of the collapsing studio system, these new low-budget films could afford to take risks and explore new artistic territory outside of the classical Hollywood narrative. Maya Deren was soon joined in New York by a crowd of like minded avant-garde filmmakers who were interested in creating films as works of art rather than entertainment. Based upon a common belief that the "official cinema" was "running out of breath" and had become "morally corrupt, aesthetically obsolete, thematically superficial, [and] temperamentally boring,",[8] this new crop of independents formed The Film-Makers' Cooperative, an artist-run, non-profit organization which they would use to distribute their films through a centralized archive. Founded in 1962 by Jonas Mekas, Stan Brakhage, Shirley Clarke, Gregory Markopoulos, and others, the Cooperative provided an important outlet for many of cinema's creative luminaries in the 1960s, including Jack Smith and Andy Warhol. When he returned to America, Ken Anger would debut many of his most important works there. Mekas and Brakhage would go on to found the Anthology Film Archives in 1970, which would likewise prove essential to the development and preservation of independent films, even to this day.

The exploitation boom and the MPAA rating system

Not all low budget films existed as non-commercial art ventures. The success of films like *Little Fugitive*, which had been made with low (or sometimes non-existent) budgets encouraged a huge boom in popularity for non-studio films. Low budget film making promised exponentially greater returns (in terms of percentages) if the film could have a successful run in the theaters. During this time, independent producer/director Roger Corman began a sweeping body of work that would become legendary for its frugality and grueling shooting schedule. Until his so-called "retirement" as a director in 1971 (he continued to produce films even after this date) he would produce up to seven movies a year, matching and often exceeding the five-per-year schedule that the executives at United Artists had once thought impossible.

Like those of the avante-garde, the films of Roger Corman took advantage of the fact that unlike the studio system, independent films had never been bound by its self-imposed production code. Corman's example (and that of others like him) would help start a boom in independent B-movies in the 1960s, the principal aim of which was to bring in the youth market which the major studios had lost touch with. By promising sex, wanton violence, drug use, and nudity, these films hoped to draw audiences to independent theaters by offering to show them what the major studios could not. Horror and science fiction films experienced a period of tremendous growth during this time. As these tiny producers, theaters, and distributors continued to attempt to undercut one another, the B-grade shlock film soon fell to the level of the Z movie, a niche category of films with production values so low that they became a spectacle in their own right. The cult audiences these pictures attracted soon made them ideal candidates for midnight movie screenings revolving around audience participation and cosplay.

In 1968, a young filmmaker named George A. Romero shocked audiences with *Night of the Living Dead*, a new kind of intense and unforgiving independent horror film. This film was released just after the abandonment of the production code, but before the adoption of the MPAA rating system. As such, it was the first and last film of its kind to enjoy a completely unrestricted screening, in which young children were able to witness Romero's new brand of highly realistic gore. This film would help to set the climate of independent horror for decades to come, as films like *The Texas Chain Saw Massacre* in 1974 and *Cannibal Holocaust* in 1980 continued to push the envelope.

With the production code abandoned and violent and disturbing films like Romero's gaining popularity, Hollywood opted to placate the uneasy filmgoing public with the MPAA ratings system, which would place restrictions on ticket sales to young people. Unlike the production code, this rating system posed a threat to independent films in that it would affect the number of tickets they could sell and cut into the grindhouse cinema's share of the youth market. This change would further widen the divide between commercial and non-commercial films.

New Hollywood and independent filmmaking

Following the advent of television and the Paramount Case, the major studios attempted to lure audiences with spectacle. Screen gimmicks, Widescreen processes and technical improvements, such as Cinemascope, stereo sound, 3-D and others, were invented in order to retain the dwindling audience by giving them a larger-than-life experience.

The 1950s and early 1960s saw a Hollywood dominated by musicals, historical epics, and other films which benefited from these advances. This proved commercially viable during most of the 1950s. However, by the late 1960s, audience share was dwindling at an alarming rate. Several costly flops, including *Cleopatra* and *Hello, Dolly!* put severe strain on the studios. Meanwhile, in 1951, lawyers-turned-producers Arthur Krim and Robert Benjamin had made a deal with the remaining stockholders of United Artists which would allow them to make an attempt to revive the company and, if the attempt was successful, buy it after five years. The attempt was a success, and in 1955 United Artists became the first "studio" without an actual studio. UA leased space at the Pickford/Fairbanks Studio, but did not own a studio lot as such. Because of this, many of their films would be shot on location. Primarily acting as bankers, they offered money to independent producers. Thus UA did not have the overhead, the maintenance or the expensive production staff which ran up costs at other studios. UA went public in 1956, and as the other mainstream studios fell into decline, UA prospered, adding relationships with the Mirisch brothers, Billy Wilder, Joseph E. Levine and others.

By the mid 1960s, RKO had collapsed completely, and the remaining four of big five had recognized that they did not know how to reach the youth audience. Foreign films, especially European and Japanese cinema, were experiencing a major boom in popularity with young people, who were interested in seeing films with non-traditional subjects and narrative structures. An added draw for such films was that they, like the American independents, were unencumbered by the production code. In an attempt to capture this audience, the Studios hired a host of young filmmakers (many of whom were mentored by Roger Corman) and allowed them to make their films with relatively little studio control.

In 1967, Warner Brothers offered first-time producer Warren Beatty 40% of the gross on his film *Bonnie and Clyde* instead of a minimal fee. The movie proceeded to gross over $70 million worldwide by 1973. This initial successes paved the way for the studio to relinquish almost complete control to the film school generation and began what the media dubbed "New Hollywood."

On May 16, 1969, Dennis Hopper, a young American filmmaker, wrote, directed, and acted in his first film, *Easy Rider*. Along with his producer/star/co-writer Peter Fonda, Hopper was responsible for the first completely independent film of New Hollywood. *Easy Rider* debuted at Cannes and garnered the "First Film Award," ("Prix de la premiere oeuvre") after which it received two Oscar nominations, one for best original screenplay and one for Corman-alum Jack Nicholson's breakthrough performance in the supporting role of George Hanson, an alcoholic lawyer for the American Civil Liberties Union.

Following on the heels of Easy Rider just over a week later, the revived United Artists' *Midnight Cowboy*, which, like *Easy Rider*, took numerous cues from Ken Anger and his influences in the French New Wave, became the first and only X rated film to win the Academy Award for best picture. *Midnight Cowboy* also held the distinction of featuring cameo roles by many of the top Warhol superstars, who had already become symbols of the militantly anti-Hollywood climate of NYC's independent film community.

Within a month, another young Corman trainee, Francis Ford Coppola, made his debut in Spain at the Donostia-San Sebastian International Film Festival with *The Rain People*, a film he had founded his own studio, American Zoetrope, to make a reality. Though *The Rain People* was largely overlooked by American audiences, Zoetrope would became a powerful force in New Hollywood. Through Zoetrope, Coppola formed a distribution agreement with studio giant, Warner Bros., which he would exploit to achieve wide releases for his films without making himself subject to the controlling forces of Hollywood.

These three films provided the major Hollywood studios with both an example to follow and a new crop of talent to draw from. In 1971, Zoetrope co-founder George Lucas made his feature film debut with *THX 1138*, also released by Zoetrope through their deal with Warner Bros., announcing himself as another major talent of New Hollywood. By the following year, the leaders of the New Hollywood revolution had made enough of a name for themselves that Coppola was offered Paramount's multi-generational gangster epic, *The Godfather.* Meanwhile Lucas had obtained studio funding for *American Graffiti* from Universal. In the mid-1970s, the major Hollywood studios continued to tap these new filmmakers for both ideas and personnel, producing idiosyncratic, startling original films such as *Paper Moon*, *Dog Day Afternoon* and *Taxi Driver,* all of which were met with enormous critical and commercial success. These successes by the members of New Hollywood led each of them in turn to make more and more extravagant demands, both on the studio and eventually on the audience.

It can often seem that all members of the New Hollywood generation were independent filmmakers. Though those mentioned above began with a considerable claim on the title, almost all of the major films commonly associated with the movement were studio projects. The New Hollywood generation soon became firmly entrenched in a revived incarnation of the studio system, which financed the development, production and distribution of their films. Very few of these filmmakers ever independently financed or independently released a film of their own, or ever worked on an independently financed production during the height of the generation's influence. Seemingly independent films such as *Taxi Driver*, *The Last Picture Show* and others were studio films: the scripts were based on studio pitches and subsequently paid for by the studios, the production financing was from the studio, and the marketing and distribution of the films were designed and controlled by the studio. Though Coppola made considerable efforts to resist the influence of the studios, opting to finance his risky 1979 film *Apocalypse Now* himself rather than compromise with skeptical studio executives, he, and filmmakers like him, had saved the old studios from financial ruin by providing them with a new formula for success.

Indeed, it was during this period that the very definition of an independent film became blurred. Though *Midnight Cowboy* was financed by United Artists, the company was certainly a studio. Likewise, Zoetrope was another "independent studio" which worked within the system to make a space for independent directors who needed funding. George Lucas would leave Zoetrope in 1971 to create his own independent studio, Lucasfilm, which would produce the blockbuster *Star Wars* and *Indiana Jones* franchises. In fact, the only two movies of the movement which can be described as uncompromisingly independent are *Easy Rider* at the beginning, and Peter Bogdanovich's *They All Laughed*, at the end. Peter Bogdanovich bought back the rights from the studio to his 1980 film and paid for its distribution out of his own pocket, convinced that the picture was better than what the studio believed — he eventually went bankrupt because of this.

In retrospect, it can be seen that Steven Spielberg's *Jaws* (1975) and George Lucas's *Star Wars* (1977) marked the beginning of the end for the New Hollywood. With their unprecedented box-office successes, these movies jump-started Hollywood's blockbuster mentality, giving studios a new paradigm as to how to make money in this changing commercial landscape. The focus on high-concept premises, with greater concentration on tie-in merchandise (such as toys), spin-offs into other media (such as soundtracks), and the use of sequels (which had been made more respectable by Coppola's *The Godfather Part II*), all showed the studios how to make money in the new environment.

On realizing how much money could potentially be made in films, major corporations started buying up the remaining Hollywood studios, saving them from the oblivion which befell RKO in the 50s. Eventually, even RKO was revived. The corporate mentality these companies brought to the filmmaking business would slowly squeeze out the more idiosyncratic of these young filmmakers, while ensconcing the more malleable and commercially successful of them. Like the original independents who fled the Edison Trust to form old Hollywood, the young film school graduates who had fled the studios to explore on-location shooting and dynamic, neo-realist styles and structures ended up replacing the tyrants they had sought to dislodge with a more stable and all-pervasive base of power.

Outside Hollywood

Though many of the thematic changes which would resound through the American cinema of the 1970s would prominently feature heightened depictions of realistic sex and violence, those directors who wished to reach the audience which the old Hollywood once had quickly learned to stylize these actions in a way that made them appealing and attractive, rather than repulsive or obscene. However, at the same time that the maverick film students who would become the American new wave were developing the skills they would use to take over Hollywood, many of their classmates had begun to develop in a different direction. Influenced by foreign "art house" directors, (such as Ingmar Bergman and Federico Fellini) exploitation shockers (including Joseph P. Mawra, Michael Findlay, and Henri Pachard) and those who walked the line between, (Kenneth Anger, et al.) a number of young film makers began to experiment with transgression not as a box-office draw, but as an artistic act. Directors such as John Waters and David Lynch would make a name for themselves by the early 70s for the bizarre and often disturbing imagery which characterized their films.

When Lynch's first feature film, 1977's *Eraserhead*, brought Lynch to the attention of producer Mel Brooks, he soon found himself in charge of the $5 million film *The Elephant Man* for Paramount. Though *Eraserhead* was strictly an out-of-pocket, low-budget, independent film, Lynch made the transition with unprecedented grace. The film was a huge commercial success, and earned eight Academy Award nominations, including Best Director and Best Adapted Screenplay nods for Lynch. It also established his place as a commercially viable, if somewhat dark and unconventional, Hollywood director. Seeing Lynch as a fellow studio convert, George Lucas, a fan of *Eraserhead* and now the darling of the studios, offered Lynch the opportunity to direct his next *Star Wars* sequel, *Star Wars Episode VI: Return of the Jedi.* However, Lynch had seen what had happened to Lucas and his comrades in arms after their failed attempt to do away with the studio system. He refused the opportunity, stating that he would rather work on his own projects.[9]

Lynch instead chose to direct a big budget adaptation of Frank Herbert's science fiction novel *Dune* for Italian producer Dino De Laurentiis's De Laurentiis Entertainment Group, on the condition that the company release a second Lynch project, over which the director would have complete creative control. Although De Laurentiis hoped it would be the next *Star Wars*, Lynch's *Dune* (1984) was a critical and commercial dud, costing $45 million to make, and grossing a mere $27.4 million domestically. The producer was furious that he would now be forced to allow Lynch to make any kind of film he wanted. He offered Lynch only $6 million, reasoning that it would be best to let it be a small flop and be rid of the director. However, the film, *Blue Velvet* was a resounding success. Lynch subsequently returned to his independent roots, and did not work with another major studio for over a decade.

John Waters, on the other hand, proved too hot to handle for the major studios. Distributing his films locally though a production company of his own creation known as Dreamland Productions, Waters defied the mainstream completely until the early 80s, when the fledgling New Line Cinema agreed to work with him on Polyester. During the 80s, Waters would become a pillar of the New York based independent film movement known as the "Cinema of

Transgression," a term coined by Nick Zedd in 1985 to describe a loose-knit group of like-minded New York artists using shock value and humor in their super 8mm films and video art. Other key players in this movement included Kembra Pfahler, Casandra Stark, Beth B, Tommy Turner, Richard Kern and Lydia Lunch. Rallying around such institutions as the Film-Makers' Cooperative and Anthology Film Archives, this new generation of independents devoted themselves to the defiance of the now-establishment New Hollywood, proposing that "all film schools be blown up and all boring films never be made again."[10]

The Sundance Institute

In 1978, Sterling Van Wagenen and Charles Gary Allison, with Chairperson Robert Redford, (veteran of New Hollywood and star of *Butch Cassidy and the Sundance Kid*) founded the Utah/US Film Festival in an effort to attract more filmmakers to Utah and showcase what the potential of independent film could be. At the time, the main focus of the event was to present a series of retrospective films and filmmaker panel discussions; however it also included a small program of new independent films. The jury of the 1978 festival was headed by Gary Allison, and included Verna Fields, Linwood Gale Dunn, Katherine Ross, Charles E. Sellier Jr., Mark Rydell, and Anthea Sylbert.

In 1981, the same year that United Artists, bought out by MGM, ceased to exist as a venue for independent filmmakers, Sterling Van Wagenen left the film festival to help found the Sundance Institute with Robert Redford. In 1985, the now well-established Sundance Institute, headed by Sterling Van Wagenen, took over management of the US Film Festival, which was experiencing financial difficulties. Gary Beer and Sterling Van Wagenen spearheaded production of the inaugural Sundance Film Festival which included Program Director Tony Safford and Administrative Director Jenny Walz Selby.

In 1991, the festival was officially renamed the *Sundance Film Festival*, after Redford's famous role as The Sundance Kid.[11] Through this festival, such notable figures as Kevin Smith, Robert Rodriguez, Quentin Tarantino, Paul Thomas Anderson, Steven Soderbergh, James Wan and Jim Jarmusch garnered resounding critical acclaim and unprecedented box office sales. In 2005, about 15% of the U.S. domestic box office revenue was from independent studios.[12]

The "Indie Film" Movement

The 1990s saw the rise and success of independent films not only through the film festival circuit but at the box office as well while established actors, such as Bruce Willis, John Travolta, and Tim Robbins, found success themselves both in independent films and Hollywood studio films.[13] The success of *Teenage Mutant Ninja Turtles* in 1990 from New Line Cinema grossed over $100 million in the United States making it the most successful indie film in box-office history.[14] Miramax Films had a string of hits with *Sex, Lies, and Videotape*, *My Left Foot: The Story of Christy Brown*, and *Cinema Paradiso*, putting Miramax and New Line Cinema in the sights of big companies looking to cash in on the success of independent studios. In 1993, Disney bought Miramax for $60 million. Turner Broadcasting, in a billion-dollar deal, acquired New Line Cinema, Fine Line Features, and Castle Rock Entertainment in 1994. The acquisitions proved to be a good move for Turner Broadcasting as New Line released *The Mask* and *Dumb & Dumber*, Castle Rock released *The Shawshank Redemption*, and Miramax released *Pulp Fiction*, all in 1994.[14]

The acquisitions of the smaller studios by conglomerate Hollywood was a plan in part to take over the independent film industry and at the same time start independent studios of their own. The following are all indie studios owned by conglomerate Hollywood:

- Sony Pictures Classics 1992
- Fox Searchlight Pictures 1995
- Paramount Vantage 1998
- Focus Features 2002

- Warner Independent Pictures 2003 [15]

By the early 2000s, Hollywood was producing three different classes of films: 1) Big Budget Blockbusters 2) Art films, specialty films and niche-market films produced by the conglomerate-owned indies and 3) Genre and specialty films coming from true indie studios and producers. The third category comprised over half the features released in the United States and usually cost between $5 and $10 million to produce.[16]

Hollywood was producing three different classes of feature films by means of three different types of producers. The superior products were the large, budget blockbusters and high-cost star vehicles marketed by the six major studio producer-distributors. Budgets on the major studios' pictures averaged $100 million, with approximately one-third spent of it spent on marketing because of the large release campaigns. Another class of Hollywood feature film included art films, specialty films, and other niche-market fare controlled by the conglomerates' indie subsidiaries. Budgets on these indie films averaged $40 million per release in the early 2000s, with $10 million to $15 million spent on marketing (MPA, 2006:12). The final class of film consisted of genre and specialty films administered by independent producer-distributors with only a few dozen or possibly a few hundred-release campaigns screens in select urban markets. Films like these usually cost less than $10 million, but frequently less than $5 million, with small marketing budgets that escalate if and when a particular film performs. [17]

Present day and digital filmmaking

Today, due to the large volume of inexpensive, high end digital film equipment available at the consumer level, independent filmmakers are no longer dependent on major studios to provide them with the tools they need to produce a film. Thanks to the falling cost of technology, thousands of small production companies can obtain the resources they need to produce entertaining films at a fraction of the cost of the big Hollywood studios. Post production has also been simplified by non-linear editing software available for home computers.

Presently, five of the Golden Age Majors continue to exist as important Hollywood studio entities through 2009. Their output is still marked by familiar stories and conservative choices in cast and crew. Companies such as Lucasfilm continue to exist, co-financing their productions and partnering with Big Six studios for distribution. In fact, co-financing has become a growing trend in modern day Hollywood, with over two-thirds of the films put out by Warner Bros. in 2000 being funded as joint ventures, up from 10% in 1987.[18]

In an effort to cash in on the present day boom in independent film, today's Big Six major studios have created a number of independent-flavored subsidiaries, designed to develop less commercial, more character driven films which appeal to the growing art house market. These include MGM, UA (under MGM), New Line Cinema, HBO Films, Castle Rock Entertainment, Disneynature, DreamWorks, Sony Pictures Classics, Fox Searchlight Pictures, Miramax Films, Warner Independent Pictures, Picturehouse, Paramount Classics/Paramount Vantage, Go Fish Pictures (under DreamWorks), Focus Features, Screen Gems, TriStar Pictures, Destination Films, Fox Faith, Fox Atomic, Gener8Xion Entertainment, Hollywood Pictures, Rogue Pictures and Sherwood Pictures.

The increasing popularity and feasibility of low-budget films over the last 15 years has led to a vast increase in the number of aspiring filmmakers — people who have written spec scripts and who hope to find several million dollars to turn that script into a successful independent film like *Reservoir Dogs, Little Miss Sunshine,* or *Juno*. Aspiring filmmakers often work day-jobs while they pitch their scripts to independent film production companies, talent agents, and wealthy investors. Their dreams are much more attainable than they were before the independent film revolution because gaining the backing of a major studio is no longer needed in order for aspiring filmmakers to potentially access millions of dollars to make their film.

Independent movie-making has also resulted in the proliferation and repopularization of short films and short film festivals. Full-length films are often showcased at film festivals such as the Sundance Film Festival, the Slamdance Film Festival, the South By Southwest film festival, the Raindance Film Festival, ACE Film Festival, or the Cannes Film Festival. Award winners from these exhibitions are more likely to get picked up for distribution by major film studios.

The following studios are considered to be the most prevalent of the modern independent studios (they are used to produce/release independent films and foreign-language films in America):

- Film4 Productions
- Lions Gate Films
- Summit Entertainment
- Overture Films
- Hannover House
- IFC Films
- Samuel Goldwyn Films
- The Weinstein Company/Dimension Films
- Magnolia Pictures
- Palm Pictures
- Tartan Films
- Newmarket Films
- ThinkFilm
- Troma Entertainment
- Maverick Entertainment Group
- First Look Studios
- Image Entertainment
- Maya Entertainment
- Entertainment One
- Phase 4 Films
- Yari Film Group
- Screen Media Films
- LD Entertainment

In addition to these higher profile "independent" studios there are thousands of smaller production companies that produce authentic independent films every year. These smaller companies look to regionally release their films theatrically or for additional financing and resources to distribute, advertise and exhibit their project on a national scale. The direct-to-video market is not often noted as artistically fertile ground but among its many entries are ambitious independent films that either failed to achieve theatrical distribution or did not seek it. Moving forward, particularly as theatrical filming goes digital and distribution eventually follows, the line between "film," direct-to-disc productions, and feature-length videos whose main distribution channel is wholly electronic, should continue to blur.

Technology and independent films today

The independent film scene's development in the 1990s and 2000s has been stimulated by a range of factors, including the development of affordable digital cinematography cameras that can rival 35 mm film quality and easy-to-use computer editing software. Until digital alternatives became available, the cost of professional film equipment and stock was a major obstacle to independent filmmakers who wanted to make their own films. In 2002, the cost of 35 mm film stock went up 23%, according to *Variety*.[18]

With the advent of consumer camcorders in 1985, and more importantly, the arrival of digital video in the early 1990s lowered the technology barrier to movie production. The personal computer and non-linear editing system have dramatically reduced costs of post-production, while technologies such as DVD, Blu-ray Disc and online video services have simplified distribution. Even 3-D technology is available to low-budget, independent filmmakers now.

With new technology, such as the Arri Alexa, RED Epic, and the many new DSLRs, independent films can create footage that looks like 35mm film without the same high cost. These cameras also perform well in low light situations. In 2008 Canon released the first DSLR camera that could shoot full HD video, the Canon EOS 5D Mark II. With the creation of the 5D Mark II, and subsequent DSLRs capable of video, independent filmmakers have the ability to shoot 1080p video at 24fps, which is considered the standard for 'film'.[19] Also these DSLRs allow for a greater control over depth of field, great low light capabilities, and a large variety of exchangeable lenses — things which independent filmmakers have been longing for for years.[20]

In addition to new digital cameras, independent film makers are benefitting from the new editing software. Instead of needing a post-house to do the editing, independent film makers can now use a personal computer and cheap editing software to edit their films. Editing software available include Avid Media Composer, Adobe Premiere Pro, Final Cut Pro, (Color Grading Software) DaVinci Resolve, and many more. These new technologies allow independent film makers to create films that are comparable to high-budget films.

Director Francis Ford Coppola, long an advocate of new technologies like non-linear editing and digital cameras, said in 2007 that "cinema is escaping being controlled by the financier, and that's a wonderful thing. You don't have to go hat-in-hand to some film distributor and say, 'Please will you let me make a movie?'"[21]

See also

- Low budget film
- No budget film
- underground film
- List of film festivals
- Film Festivals
- Art film, also known as "arthouse films" or "art cinema"
- Major Movie Studios
- The Movie Making Manual wikibook
- list of video topics
- Video
- Chroma key
- History of cinema
- List of 'years in film'
- Silent movies
- Talkies
- Independent Spirit Awards

References

[1] "Indie Film Financing makeindependentfilms.com" (http://www.makeindependentfilms.com/financing.htm). 2007. . Retrieved 2011-09-12.

[2] "La-La Land: The Origins" Peter Edidin. *New York Times*. New York, N.Y.: August 21, 2005. pg. 4.2. "Los Angeles's distance from New York was also comforting to independent film producers, making it easier for them to avoid being harassed or sued by the Motion Picture Patents Company, AKA the Trust, which Thomas Edison helped create in 1909."

[3] Siklos, Richard (March 4, 2007). Mission Improbable: Tom Cruise as Mogul. *New York Times*

[4] "The Sight & Sound Top Ten Poll: 1992" (http://www.bfi.org.uk/sightandsound/topten/history/1992.html). *Sight & Sound*. British Film Institute. . Retrieved 2008-05-20.

[5] "Take One: The First Annual Village Voice Film Critics' Poll" (http://web.archive.org/web/20070826201343/http://www.villagevoice.com/specials/take/one/full_list.php3?category=10). *The Village Voice*. 1999. Archived from the original (http://www.villagevoice.com/specials/take/one/full_list.php3?category=10) on 2007-08-26. . Retrieved 2006-07-27.

[6] The Best 1,000 Movies Ever Made (http://www.nytimes.com/ref/movies/1000best.html) By THE FILM CRITICS OF THE NEW YORK TIMES, New York Times, 2002.

[7] "All-time 100 Movies" (http://www.time.com/time/2005/100movies/the_complete_list.html). *Time* (Time Inc). 2005. . Retrieved 2008-05-19.

[8] History (http://www.film-makerscoop.com/history.htm)

[9] http://www.davidlynch.de/tiplynchtrans.html

[10] http://www.ubu.com/film/transgression.html

[11] Lauren David Peden (December 2005). "Sundance Subdued" (http://web.archive.org/web/20070927202623/http://www.coastmagazine.com/archive/pre_dec05/travel_sundance.html). Freedom Orange County Information (coastmagazine.com). Archived from the original (http://www.coastmagazine.com/archive/pre_dec05/travel_sundance.html) on 2007-09-27. . Retrieved 2007-11-11.

[12] MPAA data from January too March 2005

[13] Levy, Emanuel. Cinema of Outsiders : The Rise of American Independent Film. New York, NY, USA: NYU Press, 1999. p 13-14.

[14] McDonald, Paul and Wasco, Janet. The Contemporary Hollywood Film Industry. Malden, MA, USA: Blackwell Publishing, 2008. p 29

[15] McDonald, Paul and Wasco, Janet. The Contemporary Hollywood Film Industry. Malden, MA, USA: Blackwell Publishing, 2008. p 29-30

[16] McDonald, Paul and Wasco, Janet. The Contemporary Hollywood Film Industry. Malden, MA, USA: Blackwell Publishing, 2008. p 30-31

[17] McDonald, Paul and Wasco, Janet. The Contemporary Hollywood Film Industry. Malden, MA, USA: Blackwell Publishing, 2008. p.31

[18] Sharing Pix is Risky Business (http://www.variety.com/index.asp?layout=print_story&articleid=VR1117895718&categoryid=10) variety.com. Retrieved June 23, 2007.

[19] http://www.filmmaking.net/faq/answers/faq172.asp

[20] Eric Escobar from NAB, We Are All Geeks Now

[21] Kirsner, Scott (2008). *Inventing the Movies: Hollywood's Epic Battle Between Innovation and the Status Quo, from Thomas Edison to Steve Jobs* (http://www.scottkirsner.com/inventing). Boston, MA: CinemaTech Books. p. 199. ISBN 1438209991. .

Further reading

- Lyons, Donald (1994). *Independent Visions: A Critical Introduction to Recent Independent American Film.* Ballantine Books. ISBN 0-345-38249-8.
- Vachon, Christine (1996). *A Killer Life: How an Independent Film Producer Survives Deals and Disasters in Hollywood and Beyond.* Simon & Schuster. ISBN 0-7432-5630-1.
- Redding, Judith; Brownworth, Victoria (1997). *Film Fatales: Independent Women Directors.* Seal Press. ISBN 1-878067-97-4.
- Levy, Emanuel (1999). *Cinema of Outsiders: The Rise of American Independent Film.* New York University Press. ISBN 0-8147-5123-7.
- Merritt, Greg (2000). *Celluloid Mavericks: The History of American Independent Film.* Thunder's Mouth Press. ISBN 1-56025-232-4.
- Biskind, Peter (2004). *Down and Dirty Pictures: Miramax, Sundance, and the Rise of Independent Film.* Simon & Schuster. ISBN 0-684-86259-X.
- Pierson, John (2004). *Spike Mike Reloaded.* Miramax Books. ISBN 1-4013-5950-7.
- Levy, Emanuel (2001). *Cinema of Outsiders: The Rise of American Independent Film.* NYU Press. ISBN 978-0814751244.
- Hall, Phil (2009). *The History of Independent Cinema.* BearManor Media. ISBN 1593933355.
- Richard Dyer Maccann (Summer, 1962). "Independence, with a Vengeance". *Film Quarterly* (University of California Press) **15** (4): 14–21. doi:10.1525/fq.1962.15.4.04a00060. JSTOR 1211185.

External links

- IFTA (http://www.afma.com/) - The Independent Film & Television Alliance, an International trade association representing Independent Producers
- Indie Films (http://indie.imdb.com/index.indie) at the Internet Movie Database
- Independent Feature Project (http://www.ifp.org) IFP
- Indie Horror Comedy (http://www.hellphone.com) at Hellphone -Indie Horror Comedy

Sundance_Film_Festival

Sundance Film Festival	

Location	Park City, Utah, United States
Language	International
http://festival.sundance.org/	

The **Sundance Film Festival** is an American film festival that takes place annually in Utah. It is the largest independent cinema festival in the United States.[1] Held in January in Park City, Salt Lake City, and Ogden, as well as at the Sundance Resort, the festival is a showcase for new work from American and international independent filmmakers. The festival comprises competitive sections for American and international dramatic and documentary films, both feature-length films and short films, and a group of out-of-competition sections, including NEXT, New Frontier, Spotlight, and Park City At Midnight.

History

Utah/US Film Festival

Sundance began in Salt Lake City in August 1978, as the Utah/US Film Festival in an effort to attract more filmmakers to Utah. It was founded by Sterling Van Wagenen (then head of Wildwood, Robert Redford's company), John Earle, and Cirina Hampton Catania (both serving on the Utah Film Commission at the time). The 1978 festival featured films such as *Deliverance*, *A Streetcar Named Desire*, *Midnight Cowboy*, *Mean Streets*, and *The Sweet Smell of Success*. [2] With Chairperson Robert Redford, and the help of Governor Scott M. Matheson of Utah, the goal of the festival was to showcase strictly American-made films, highlight the potential of independent film, and to increase visibility for filmmaking in Utah. At the time, the main focus of the event was to conduct a competition for independent American films, present a series of retrospective films and filmmaker panel discussions, and to celebrate the Frank Capra Award. The festival also highlighted the work of regional filmmakers who worked outside the Hollywood system.

The jury of the 1978 festival was headed by Gary Allison, and included Verna Fields, Linwood G. Dunn, Katharine Ross, Charles E. Sellier Jr., Mark Rydell, and Anthea Sylbert.

In 1979, Sterling Van Wagenen left to head up the first year "pilot" program of what was to become the Sundance Institute, and Cirina Hampton Catania took over as executive director of the festival. Over 60 films were screened at the festival that year, and panels featured many well-known Hollywood filmmakers. Also that year, the first Frank Capra Award went to Jimmy Stewart. The festival also made a profit for the first time. In 1980, Catania left the festival to pursue a production career in Hollywood.

Several factors helped propel the growth of Utah/US Film Festival. First was the involvement of actor and Utah resident Robert Redford, who became the festival's inaugural chairman. By having Redford's name associated with

Sundance, the festival received great attention. Secondly, the country was hungry for more venues that would celebrate American-made films as the only other festival doing so at the time was the USA Film Festival in Dallas (est. 1971). Response in Hollywood was unprecedented as major studios did all they could to contribute their resources.

In 1981, the festival moved to Park City, Utah, and changed the dates from September to January. The move from late summer to mid-winter was reportedly done on the advice of Hollywood director Sydney Pollack, who suggested that running a film festival in a ski resort during winter would draw more attention from Hollywood.

Change to Sundance

In 1984–85, the now well-established Sundance Institute, headed by Sterling Van Wagenen, took over management of the US Film Festival and changed the name to Sundance. Gary Beer and Sterling Van Wagenen spearheaded production of the inaugural Sundance Film Festival, which included Program Director Tony Safford and Administrative Director Jenny Walz Selby. The branding and marketing transition from the U.S. Film Festival to the Sundance Film Festival was managed under the direction of Colleen Allen, Allen Advertising Inc., by appointment of Robert Redford.

Sundance London

In March 2011, Robert Redford announced that the Sundance Film Festival would be held at The O2, in London from 26th – 29th April 2012, the first time it has travelled outside the United States.

Speaking to the press, Redford said, "We are excited to partner with AEG Europe to bring a particular slice of American culture to life in the inspired setting of The O2, and in this city of such rich cultural history. [...] It is our mutual goal to bring to the UK, the very best in current American independent cinema, to introduce the artists responsible for it, and in essence help build a picture of our country that is broadly reflective of the diversity of voices not always seen in our cultural exports."

The majority of the film screenings, including the festival's premieres, will be held within the Cineworld cinema.[3]

Sundance Institute

Management of the festival was taken over by the Sundance Institute, a non-profit organization, in 1985. In 1991 the festival was officially renamed the *Sundance Film Festival*, after Redford's character The Sundance Kid from the movie *Butch Cassidy and the Sundance Kid*.[4]

From 2006 through 2008, the Sundance Institute collaborated with the Brooklyn Academy of Music (BAM) on a special series of film screenings, performances, panel discussions, and special events bringing the institute's activities and the festival's programming to New York City.[5]

Notability of festivals

Many famous independent filmmakers received their big break at Sundance, including Kevin Smith, Robert Rodriguez, Quentin Tarantino, Todd Field, Steve James, Paul Thomas Anderson, Steven Soderbergh, Darren Aronofsky, James Wan, Edward Burns, and Jim Jarmusch. The festival is also responsible for bringing wider attention to such films as *Saw*, *Garden State*, *Super Troopers*, *The Blair Witch Project*, *Better Luck Tomorrow*, *Primer*, *Reservoir Dogs*, *In the Bedroom*, *Little Miss Sunshine*, *El Mariachi*, *Moon*, *Clerks*, *Thank You for Smoking*, *Sex, Lies, and Videotape*, *The Brothers McMullen*, and *Napoleon Dynamite*.

Three Seasons was the first in festival history to ever receive both the Grand Jury Award and Audience Award, in 1999. Later films that won both awards are: *God Grew Tired of Us* in 2006 (documentary category), *Quinceañera* in 2006 (dramatic category), and *Precious* in 2009.

At the 2010 Sundance Film Festival, 9 films went on to garner 15 Oscar nominations,[6] and 4 of the 5 Best Documentary nominees were Sundance films.[7] The next year, about 45 films were acquired by distributors (the most ever[8]) vs. 14 in 2010, an increase of about 220%.[9] Tom Hall of indieWire said it marked "a return to the glory days of pure, unadulterated content speculation."[10]

Growth of the festival

The festival has changed over the decades from a low-profile venue for small-budget, independent creators from outside the Hollywood system to a media extravaganza for Hollywood celebrity actors, paparazzi, and luxury lounges set up by companies not affiliated with Sundance. Festival organizers have tried curbing these activities in recent years, beginning in 2007 with their ongoing "Focus On Film" campaign.

Included in the changes made in 2010, a new programming category, "NEXT," is for extremely low-budget films. Another change includes the Sundance Film Festival U.S.A. program, in which eight of the festival's films will be shown in eight theaters around the country.[11]

Directors

- Geoff Gilmore – 1991–2009[12] [13]
- John Cooper — March 2009[14]

In popular culture

In August 1998, the animated television series *South Park* episode "Chef's Chocolate Salty Balls" depicts the directors of the Sundance Festival moving it to a "different small mountain town," that of the show's main setting South Park, in order to "drain it and morph it into a new LA."

In the television series *Entourage*, one of the independent movies which Vincent Chase stars in (*Queens Boulevard*) premieres at the Sundance Film Festival, where it begins to gain in popularity.

In animated television series *The Simpsons* episode "Any Given Sundance," Lisa Simpson enters a documentary about her family into the Sundance Film Festival.

In Season 7, Episode 22 of *One Tree Hill*, Julian Baker takes his film 'Seven Days Till Tuesday' to the festival.

See also

- List of Sundance Film Festival award winners
- List of Sundance Film Festival selections
- Sundance Channel
- Sundance Institute

References

Notes

[1] The Associated Press (January 18, 2006). "Sundance Mixed With Stars, Politicians" (http://movies.yahoo.com/mv/sundance/news/aps/20060118/113762388000.html). via Yahoo! News. . Retrieved 2007-11-11.

[2] Sundance-A Festival Virgin's Guide: History of the Sundance Film Festival; www.sundanceguide.net/basics/history

[3] "Robert Redford, Sundance Institute and AEG Europe launch Sundance London at The O2" (http://www.sundance-london.com/news/20110315-sundance-london-announced-at-the-o2). Sundance London. . Retrieved 19 January 2012.

[4] Lauren David Peden (December 2005). "Sundance Subdued" (http://web.archive.org/web/20070927202623/http://www.coastmagazine.com/archive/pre_dec05/travel_sundance.html). Freedom Orange County Information (coastmagazine.com). Archived from the original (http://www.coastmagazine.com/archive/pre_dec05/travel_sundance.html) on 2007-09-27. . Retrieved 2007-11-11.

[5] "Sundance Mixed With Stars, Politicians" (http://www.bam.org/sundance/index_2007.aspx). BAM. . Retrieved 2007-11-11.

[6] Dana Harris (January 25, 2011). "The 15 Oscar Nominees That Came Out of Sundance 2010" (http://www.indiewire.com/article/the_14_oscar_nominees_that_came_out_of_sundance/). *indieWire*. . Retrieved February 4, 2011.
[7] Peter Knegt (February 3, 2011). "For Your Consideration: Sundance and Next Year's Oscars" (http://www.indiewire.com/article/for_your_consideration_sundance_and_next_years_oscars1/). *indieWire*. . Retrieved February 4, 2011.
[8] Jada Yuan (January 30, 2011). "Like Crazy's Big Win, and Other Highlights From the Sundance Awards Ceremony" (http://nymag.com/daily/entertainment/2011/01/sundance_2.html?imw=Y&f=most-viewed-24h5). *New York*. . Retrieved February 4, 2011.
[9] Alicia Rancilio (January 30, 2011). "Redford relieved this year's Sundance is ending" (http://www.seattlepi.com/movies/1402ap_us_sundance_robert_redford.html). *Associated Press*. . Retrieved February 4, 2011.
[10] Tom Hall (January 29, 2011). "Sundance 2011" (http://blogs.indiewire.com/twhalliii/archives/2011/01/29/sundance_2011_the_market_is_now_open/). *indieWire*. . Retrieved February 4, 2011.
[11] "Redford launches 2010 Sundance Film Festival in Park City" (http://heraldextra.com/news/local/article_38fab10a-0120-5c9a-bec2-b0c13dc56df8.html). The Daily Herald. 2010. . Retrieved 2010-01-22.
[12] Jeremy Kay (2009) John Cooper steps up as director of Sundance Film Festival (http://www.screendaily.com/john-cooper-steps-up-as-director-of-sundance-film-festival/4043584.article), 11 March 2009, ScreenDaily.com. Retrieved on 2010-01-31.
[13] Michael Cieply (2009) Shakeup in Film Festivals as a Familiar Face Moves (http://www.nytimes.com/2009/02/18/movies/18tribeca.html), 17 February 2009, The New York Times. Retrieved on 2010-01-31.
[14] Sundance Institute (2009) Sundance Institute announces John Cooper as Director, Sundance Film Festival (http://www.sundance.org/pdf/2009-03-09-cooper.pdf), Press release, 11 March 2009, www.sundance.org. Retrieved on 2010-01-31.

2. Benjamin Craig, "Sundance-A Festival Virgin's Guide: History of the Sundance Film Festival," www.sundanceguide.net/basics/history

Further reading

- Biskind, Peter. *Down and Dirty Pictures: Miramax, Sundance, and the Rise of Independent Film*. Simon & Schuster, 2004.
- Smith, Lory. *Party in a Box: The Story of the Sundance Film Festival* . Gibbs Smith Publishers, 1999.
- Craig, Benjamin. *Sundance — A Festival Virgin's Guide*. Cinemagine Media Publishing, 2004.
- Anderson, John. *Sundancing: Hanging Out And Listening In At America's Most Important Film Festival*. Harper Paperbacks, 2000.

External links

- Official website (http://http://www.sundance.org/)
- Sundance – A Festival Virgin's Guide (http://www.sundanceguide.net/) – detailed festival history and information for attendees.
- Festival Guide (http://www.indiewire.com/festival/sundance_film_festival/) – Indie film resource
- LA Times article on 2010 competition films (http://latimesblogs.latimes.com/awards/2009/12/2010-sundance-film-festival-announces-film-lineup.html)
- Photos from Sundance Film Festival 2010 (http://www.mynorthwest.com/?sid=276160&nid=643) (January 26, 2010)

Bad_Robot_Productions

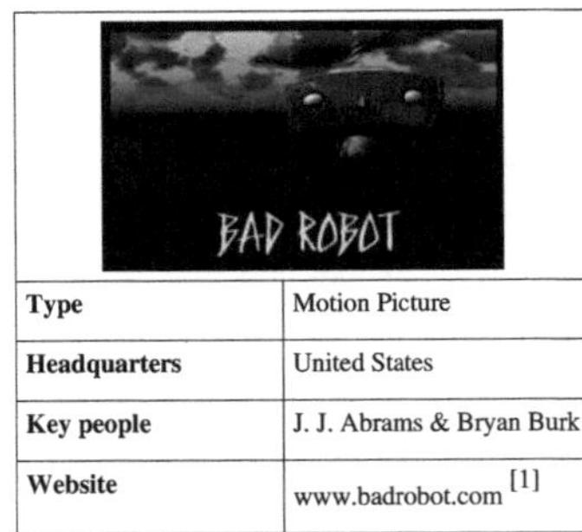

Type	Motion Picture
Headquarters	United States
Key people	J. J. Abrams & Bryan Burk
Website	www.badrobot.com [1]

Bad Robot Productions (formerly known as only **Bad Robot**) is an American film and television production company owned by J. J. Abrams. It is responsible for the television series *Alias*, *Lost*, *What About Brian*, *Six Degrees*, *Fringe*, *Undercovers*, *Person of Interest* and *Alcatraz* and the feature length films *Cloverfield*, *Star Trek*, *Super 8*, and *Mission: Impossible – Ghost Protocol*.[2]

Bad Robot was originally part of Touchstone Television, but has moved with J. J. Abrams to Paramount Pictures and Warner Bros. Television, after his contract with Touchstone had expired in 2006. Bad Robot produced *Lost* in association with ABC Studios, formerly Touchstone Television. The two companies jointly produced *Six Degrees* and *What About Brian*.

Abrams is Chairman/Chief Executive Officer, and Bryan Burk serves as Executive Vice President of the company.

The production logo has appeared since 2001, featuring a red rectangular headed robot running through a meadow silhouetted until it appears suddenly in front of the camera, followed by voices provided by two of Abrams' children, Henry and Gracie Abrams, saying "Bad robot!"[3]

Productions

Bad Robot Productions produces both television programs and films.

The original Bad Robot Productions logo used from 2001 to 2008, though still used on the company's website.

Films

Year	Title	Notes	Budget	Gross
2001	*Joy Ride*	Co-production with 20th Century Fox and Regency Enterprises	$23 million	$36,642,838
2006	*Mission: Impossible III*	Co-production with Paramount Pictures and Cruise/Wagner Productions	$150 million	$397,850,012
2008	*Cloverfield*	Co-production with Paramount Pictures	$25 million	$170,764,026
2009	*Star Trek*	Co-production with Paramount Pictures and Spyglass Entertainment	$150 million	$385,680,446
2010	*Morning Glory*	Co-production with Paramount Pictures	$40 million	$58,785,180
2011	*Super 8*	Co-production with Paramount Pictures and Amblin Entertainment	$50 million	$259,422,500
2011	*Mission: Impossible – Ghost Protocol*	Co-production with Paramount Pictures and Skydance Productions	$145 million	$693,054,071
2013	Untitled *Star Trek* sequel	Co-production with Paramount Pictures and Skydance Productions, upcoming		

TV series

Year	Title	Notes
2001–2006	*Alias*	
2004–2010	*Lost*	
2005	*The Catch*	Pilot
2006–2007	*What About Brian*	
2006–2007	*Six Degrees*	
Since 2008	*Fringe*	
2009	*Anatomy of Hope*	Pilot
2010	*Undercovers*	
Since 2011	*Person of Interest*	
2012	*Alcatraz*	
Since 2012	*Revolution* [4]	

Awards and recognition

- 2002 Emmy Award Nomination, Outstanding Writing for A Drama Series (*Alias*)
- **2005 Emmy Award Winner, Outstanding Drama Series (*Lost*)**
- **2005 Emmy Award Winner, Outstanding Directing for A Drama Series (*Lost*)**
- 2005 Emmy Award Nomination, Outstanding Writing for A Drama Series (*Lost*)
- **2006 Golden Globe Award Winner, Best Television Series - Drama (*Lost*)**
- 2007 Golden Globe Award Nomination, Best Television Series - Drama (*Lost*)

References

[1] http://www.badrobot.com/

[2] http://www.enotes.com/topic/Bad_Robot_Productions, Enotes

[3] Nicholas Fonseca (2001-12-07). "'Alias': The Story Behind J.J. Abrams' Bad Robot" (http://www.ew.com/ew/article/0,,253033,00.html). *Entertainment Weekly*. . Retrieved 2012-03-22.

[4] http://www.deadline.com/2012/05/save-me-picked-up-to-series-as-nbc-starts-new-series-pickup/

External links

- Official website (http://http://www.badrobot.com/)
- "Bad Robot Productions Signs Far-Reaching Production Deals With Columbia Pictures, Paramount Pictures and Warner Bros. Television" (http://www.timewarner.com/corp/newsroom/pr/0,20812,1215680,00.html) (Press release). Time Warner. 2006-07-15.
- Andreeva, Nellie; Tatiana Siegel (2006-07-17). "Abrams builds his Robot" (http://www.hollywoodreporter.com/hr/search/article_display.jsp?vnu_content_id=1002839924). *The Hollywood Reporter*.

Spyglass_Entertainment

The current Spyglass Entertainment logo

Type	Private
Industry	Film
Predecessor(s)	Caravan Pictures
Founded	1998
Founder(s)	Gary Barber Roger Birnbaum
Headquarters	Los Angeles, California, United States
Key people	Jeffrey Chernov Jonathan Glickman
Products	Motion pictures
Parent	Cerberus Capital Management
Website	www.spyglassentertainment.com [1]

Spyglass Entertainment is an American film production company, co-founded by Gary Barber and Roger Birnbaum in 1998.[2] The studio was founded with an investment from European media conglomerates Kirch Group and Mediaset,[3] and a five-year distribution deal with The Walt Disney Company.[4] It is currently owned by Cerberus Capital Management.

Barber and Birnbaum serve as co-CEOs, while Jonathan Glickman serves as the current President of Production. Jeffrey Chernov was once a production executive at Spyglass Entertainment.

Spyglass Entertainment is expected to finalize a deal to take over 5% of Metro-Goldwyn-Mayer.[5] [6]

The MGM creditors have approved the Spyglass Entertainment plan.[7] [8] [9] [10]

On November 3, 2010, MGM filed for Chapter 11 bankruptcy.[11] [12] [13] MGM emerged from bankruptcy on December 20, 2010, at which time the founders of Spyglass Entertainment, Gary Barber and Roger Birnbaum, became co-Chairs and co-CEOs of the holding company of Metro-Goldwyn-Mayer.[14] [14] [14] [14]

UK Distributors

- Buena Vista International (2002-2005)
- Optimum Releasing (2009-2011)
- StudioCanal UK (2011-present)

Production filmography

1990s

- *Instinct* (1999) (co-production with Touchstone Pictures)
- *The Sixth Sense* (1999) (co-production with Hollywood Pictures, Blinding Edge Pictures and The Kennedy/Marshall Company)
- *The Insider* (1999) (co-production with Touchstone Pictures)

2000s

- *Mission to Mars* (2000) (co-production with Touchstone Pictures)
- *Keeping the Faith* (2000) (co-production with Touchstone Pictures)
- *Shanghai Noon* (2000) (co-production with Touchstone Pictures)
- *Out Cold* (2001) (co-production with Touchstone Pictures)
- *The Count of Monte Cristo* (2002) (co-production with Touchstone Pictures)
- *Dragonfly* (2002) (co-production with Universal Pictures)
- *Abandon* (2002) (co-production with Paramount Pictures)
- *Reign of Fire* (2002) (co-production with Touchstone Pictures)
- *The Recruit* (2003) (co-production with Touchstone Pictures)
- *Shanghai Knights* (2003) (co-production with Touchstone Pictures)
- *Bruce Almighty* (2003) (co-production with Universal Pictures)
- *Seabiscuit* (2003) (co-production with Universal Pictures and DreamWorks Pictures)
- *Connie and Carla* (2004) (co-production with Universal Pictures)
- *Mr. 3000* (2004) (co-production with Touchstone Pictures, Dimension Films and The Kennedy/Marshall Company)
- *The Pacifier* (2005) (co-production with Walt Disney Pictures)
- *The Hitchhiker's Guide to the Galaxy* (2005) (co-production with Touchstone Pictures and Hammer and Tongs)
- *The Legend of Zorro* (2005) (co-production with Columbia Pictures and Amblin Entertainment)
- *Memoirs of a Geisha* (2005) (co-production with Columbia Pictures, Amblin Entertainment, DreamWorks Pictures and Red Wagon Productions)
- *Eight Below* (2006) (co-production with Walt Disney Pictures, The Kennedy/Marshall Company, and Mandeville Films)
- *Stay Alive* (2006) (co-production with Hollywood Pictures and Endgame Entertainment)
- *Stick It* (2006) (co-production with Touchstone Pictures)
- *The Lookout* (2007) (co-production with Miramax Films)
- *The Invisible* (2007) (co-production with Hollywood Pictures)
- *Evan Almighty* (2007) (co-production with Universal Pictures, Relativity Media, Shady Acres Entertainment and Original Film)
- *Underdog* (2007) (co-production with Walt Disney Pictures and Classic Media)
- *Balls of Fury* (2007) (co-production with Rogue Pictures, Relativity Media and Intrepid Pictures)
- *27 Dresses* (2008) (co-production with Twentieth Century Fox)
- *Welcome Home Roscoe Jenkins* (2008) (co-production with Universal Pictures)

- *The Ruins* (2008) (co-production with DreamWorks Pictures)
- *The Happening* (2008) (co-production with Twentieth Century Fox, Blinding Edge Pictures and UTV Motion Pictures)
- *The Love Guru* (2008) (co-production with Paramount Pictures)
- *Wanted* (2008) (co-production with Universal Pictures)
- *Ghost Town* (2008) (co-production with DreamWorks Pictures)
- *Flash of Genius* (2008) (co-production with Universal Pictures and Strike Entertainment)
- *Four Christmases* (2008) (co-production with New Line Cinema)
- *Star Trek* (2009) (co-production with Paramount Pictures)
- *G.I. Joe: The Rise of Cobra* (2009) (co-production with Paramount Pictures and Hasbro)
- *Invictus* (2009) (co-production with Warner Bros. Pictures, Malpaso Productions, and Revelations Entertainment)

2010s

- *Leap Year* (2010) (co-production with Universal Pictures, Relativity Media and Optimum Releasing)
- *Get Him to the Greek* (2010) (co-production with Universal Pictures, Relativity Media and Apatow Productions)
- *Dinner for Schmucks* (2010) (co-production with Paramount Pictures and DreamWorks Pictures)
- *The Tourist* (2010) (co-production with Columbia Pictures and GK Films)
- *The Dilemma* (2011) (co-production with Universal Pictures and Imagine Entertainment)
- *No Strings Attached* (2011) (co-production with Paramount Pictures, The Montecito Picture Company and Cold Spring Pictures)
- *Footloose* (2011) (co-production with Paramount Pictures and MTV Films)
- *The Vow* (2012) (co-production with Screen Gems)
- *Hansel and Gretel: Witch Hunters* (2013) (co-production with Paramount Pictures, MGM and Gary Sanchez Productions) (last film by Spyglass Entertainment before MGM took over.)

References

[1] http://www.spyglassentertainment.com

[2] Eller, Claudia (May 23, 2000). "Spyglass Hopes for More Good 'Sense' in Future Projects" (http://articles.latimes.com/2000/may/23/business/fi-32930). *Los Angeles Times*: p. C1. . Retrieved May 12, 2010. (Alternate link (http://pqasb.pqarchiver.com/latimes/access/54077198.html?FMT=ABS&FMTS=ABS:FT).)

[3] Mattzer, Marla (October 29, 1998). "European Firms to Invest in Spyglass" (http://pqasb.pqarchiver.com/latimes/access/35507765.html?dids=35507765:35507765&FMT=ABS&FMTS=ABS:FT). *Los Angeles Times*: p. C4. . Retrieved May 12, 2010.

[4] Eller, Claudia (August 21, 1998). "Spyglass Offers Disney Lower-Risk Deals" (http://articles.latimes.com/1998/aug/21/business/fi-15109). *Los Angeles Times*: p. D5. . Retrieved May 12, 2010. (Alternate link (http://pqasb.pqarchiver.com/latimes/access/33285845.html?FMT=ABS&FMTS=ABS:FT).)

[5] MGM Has New CEOs as Spyglass Entertainment Finalizes Deal to Control the Studio (http://www.slashfilm.com/2010/10/07/mgm-has-new-ceos-as-spyglass-entertainment-finalizes-deal-to-control-the-studio), *SlashFilm*, October 7, 2010

[6] MGM Finally Files for Bankruptcy (http://blog.onthebox.com/2010/10/08/mgm-finally-file-for-bankruptcy), *On the Box*, October 8, 2010

[7] Spyglass Plan Approved By MGM Creditors (http://latimesblogs.latimes.com/entertainmentnewsbuzz/2010/10/spyglass-plan-approved-by-mgm-creditors.html), *Los Angeles Times*, October 29, 2010

[8] MGM Creditors Approve Spyglass Plan (http://www.variety.com/article/VR1118026623.html?categoryid=13&cs=1), *Variety*, October 29, 2010

[9] MGM Creditors Approve Spyglass Takeover (http://www.thewrap.com/movies/column-post/bankruptcy-vote-looms-mgms-fate-hangs-balance-22091), *The Wrap*, October 29, 2010

[10] MGM in Deal to Cut Debt (http://www.latimes.com/business/la-fi-ct-mgm-20101030,0,2264694.story), *Los Angeles Times*, October 30, 2010

[11] MGM Files Bankruptcy, Rejecting Lions Gate, Icahn Bid (http://www.businessweek.com/news/2010-11-03/mgm-files-bankruptcy-rejecting-lions-gate-icahn-bid.html), *Business Week*, November 3, 2010

[12] MGM Officially Files for Bankruptcy (http://www.thehollywoodnews.com/2010/11/03/mgm-officially-file-bankruptcy), *Hollywood News*, November 3, 2010

[13] Judge Approves MGM Bankruptcy Plan (http://www.variety.com/article/VR1118026917?refCatId=13), *Variety*, November 4, 2010

[14] "MGM 2010 Restructing" (http://online.wsj.com/public/resources/documents/CopyMGM.pdf). online.wsj.com. . Retrieved Jan 05, 2012.

External links

- Official website (http://http://www.spyglassentertainment.com)
- Spyglass Entertainment (http://www.imdb.com/company/co0031181/) at the Internet Movie Database

Article Sources and Contributors

Scenechronize *Source*: http://en.wikipedia.org/w/index.php?title=Scenechronize *Contributors*: Bearcat, CAWylie

Computing_platform *Source*: http://en.wikipedia.org/w/index.php?title=Computing_platform *Contributors*: 123Hedgehog456, Acjelen, Ae-a, Ahoerstemeier, Andareed, Andrea105, Anthony Appleyard, Armando, Askari786, Ayda D, BarretB, Benlisquare, Benzband, Blue520, Bobo192, Bovineone, CanisRufus, Cgs, Chekristo, ChrisGualtieri, Cleduc, Cogiati, Conti, Control.optimization, CoolingGibbon, Cpiral, CyberSkull, Daclyff, DarkOne, David A Bozzini, Dcirovic, Diacspaa, Dipskinny, Dmsar, DocWatson42, Donnay, Drcwright, Dysprosia, Electron9, Esebi95, Ffaarr, Frap, Frecklefoot, Fruckert, Gadfium, Garycompugeek, Geniac, Giraffedata, Glenn4pr, Hammerhorn, Harryboyles, Hede2000, Hephaestos, Ian Bailey, Japo, Jayjg, Jerryobject, Jessemv, Jhansonxi, Jim.henderson, Jimmi Hugh, JoaoRicardo, JohnChrysostom, Jolivio, JonHarder, Jondel, Kbdank71, Kubanczyk, Kyng, Lancehyde, LeaveSleaves, Libcub, LilHelpa, Logan, MBParker, Mac, Mani1, Marko75, Martarius, Matthewrbowker, Maximus Rex, Mbaluyos, Mike Juan Lee, Mikenolte, Milly, Minesweeper, Mohmk, Moverton, Mschel, Mttcmbs, Music Sorter, Mwn3d, My wing hk, Niceguyedc, Nixdorf, Notheruser, Nuno Tavares, Nurg, Omicronpersei8, Opagecrtr, Orindlincoln, Paradoxian, Paxsimius, Piecemealcranky, Psantora, Psinu, Ptaavs, Ratchet27, Raysonho, Reisio, Rosevines, S.Örvarr.S, SF007, Sadegh87, Sega381, SemanticEngine, Slike, Ste4k, THEN WHO WAS PHONE?, Tcncv, The Anome, Triona, TutterMouse, UncleDouggie, Uzume, Van helsing, Varciasz, Vary, Vegaswikian, Warren, Wbm1058, Weregerbil, Wikidemon, Williamborg, Winterst, Yukoba, Zivorad, Zollerriia, ינ״ע לקד, 193 anonymous edits

Information_technology *Source*: http://en.wikipedia.org/w/index.php?title=Information_technology *Contributors*: .:Ajvol:., 123Hedgehog456, 24.45.80.xxx, 28421u2232nfenfcenc, 3rdiw, 7, A.arvind.arasu, A455bcd9, A8UDI, ABF, Aashaa, Abdullais4u, Academic Challenger, Accurizer, Ace of Spades, ActivExpression, AdjustShift, Admiral Roo, Adyeee, Aeternus, Agogino, AgomesNJITWILL, Ajayundale, AlMac, Alai, Alan.Ford.Jn, Alaniaris, Alansohn, Alarob, Aleenf1, Alekperova, Alexissua, AlistairMcMillan, Amorymeltzer, Anastrophe, Andonic, Andy4789, Angel14995, Angie sash, Angrysockhop, Ank329, Anna Lincoln, AnnabelBuxton, Anne97432, Antandrus, Anwar saadat, Ap, Apparition11, Arakunem, Arman Cagle, Armchairwiki, Arnon Chaffin, Arthena, Arthur Rubin, Artw, Asav, Asst2drsalary, Astudent, AtticusX, Aursani, Avjoska, Avoided, Bact, Baronnet, Be-technical, Beekers03, Beetstra, BenRG, Benhoyt, BigCow, Bilby, Billyg, BirgerH, BisKit12iNtheOven, Blanchardb, Bloodbath 87, Bobanator13, Bobo192, Bonadea, Bongomatic, Bongwarrior, Bonjour68, Brianjd, Brodger3, Bruce1ee, Bubba hotep, C messier, CBF28, CEPIS Secretariat, CS46, CZmarlin, Cafzal, Caltas, Cameron.walsh, Camw, Captain Screebo, Cbissell, Centrx, CesarB, Cessator, Cheese Sandwich, Chenzw, Chocolateboy, Chrisfro1230, Chulk90, Chuunen Baka, Citylinker, Ckatz, Claudioferreira, Colettecorr, Commander Keane, Connormah, Conversion script, Coral chernikoe, Corpx, Cpl Syx, CrashingWave, Crocodile Punter, Crysb, Cybercobra, D.h, DARTH SIDIOUS 2, DJ Bungi, DKEdwards, DVdm, Darry2385, Datajockeys, Daveniha, Davidshq, Dawynn, Delldot, DerHexer, Devin, Dfrg.msc, Diegomoranovoa, Dirtyserge, Discospinster, DocWatson42, Dockers1, Download, Dr. Sheldon Cooper, Dr.semsem85, Dragunova, Drdibendunag, Drs4ever, Ducknish, Dullhunk, Dungodung, E-Soter, ESkog, EarthPerson, EchetusXe, Edaelon, Edderso, Edinburgh Wanderer, Edjon, ElKevbo, Eliel1324, Encephalon, Epbr123, Equendil, Error -128, Escape Orbit, Espoo, Evil saltine, Exceedit, Exert, F4M, Face, Falcon8765, FayssalF, Fconaway, Finngall, Fligtar, Floodamanny, Fredrik, Fritzpoll, FullMetal Falcon, Funnybunny, GEBStgo, GQsm, GUllman, Gabbe, Gaff, Garas, Gauuzz, Giftlite, Gimboid13, Gioto, Glane23, Glenn, Gogo Dodo, Grim23, GroupOne, Gsaup, Gscshoyru, Guanaco, Guerino1, Gurchzilla, Guy Harris, Gwernol, HaeB, Haemo, Hallenrm, Halsteadk, Hamtechperson, Haphar, Happyisenough, Hard Sin, Hashp, Hawksj, Hazard-SJ, Head, Hl, Hmains, Hobartimus, Hotcrocodile, Hulagutten, I dream of horses, ITautomationFreak, Imecs, Imtiyazali4all, Informationtricks, Isheden, Ithizar, Ittarget, Ivansanchez, Ixfd64, J. W. Love, JCLately, JCasto, JD554, JForget, JaGa, Jackfork, Jake Wartenberg, James Anthony Knight, Jamessungjin.kim, Jan1nad, Jarble, Jareha, Jasper Deng, Jauhienij, Jay-Sebastos, Jayvm 10, Jeff G., Jefferycs, Jesuschex, Jettux, JhonathanZamarchi, Jim1138, JinJian, Jmax-, Jmlk17, JoWal, JoanneB, Joestansmith, Joeyd816, John, Johnchrism, Johnuniq, Jokinen, Jonomacdrones, Jorge Stolfi, Joseph Solis in Australia, Joshua, Joy, Jpbowen, Julcia, Juzeris, Kaldari, Karl-Henner, Kateshortforbob, KatherineBurris, Kenny sh, Kensor, KeyStroke, Kgfleischmann, Khalid Mahmood, Kingpin13, Kingreid8, Kku, Kne1p, Kozuch, Kreaves, Krish Dulal, Krymson, Kukini, Kuru, L Kensington, La Pianista, Laomai Weng, LcawteHuggle, LeaveSleaves, Leranedo, Leszek Jańczuk, Liempt, Liftarn, Lights, Lindengr, LittleDan, Llywelyn2000, Locutus Borg, Lollerskates, Lor772, Lord of the Pit, Loserdog3000, Lotje, Lou Crazy, Lperez2029, Lquilter, Luna Santin, Lysander89, MC10, MDE, MER-C, MK8, MMi25, Ma sassan, Mac area51, MacMed, MacTire02, Maher-shalal-hashbaz, Mahieux, Maine12329, Mako098765, Malcolma, Malleus Fatuorum, Manuel Trujillo Berges, MarSch, Marek69, Mark Renier, MarsRover, Martarius, Martin Jensen, Materialscientist, Matt Britt, Mattisse, Maurice Carbonaro, Mav, Maverick Leonhart, Mcoff, Mdd, Mejor Los Indios, Melanchthon, Melvinovski, Mentifisto, Metricopolus, Mholland, Michael Hardy, MichaelBillington, Michig, Millars, Mindmatrix, Miranda, Mitch Ames, Mitsuhara, Mohdmohsin20, Moptophaha, Morgssunflower, MosheZadka, Mr Stephen, Mr.joggee, MrOllie, Mrrogers1234, Mrzaius, Mshkc, Mtz07, Mumia-w-18, Mygerardromance, Mythdon, NZTech, Nancy, Naqsh244, Nathanael Bar-Aur L., Nathandiehl, Nayvik, Nehrams2020, Neier, Netoholic, Nicholaus Mwalukasa, Nickel&Dimed, Nitelken, Nivix, Nneonneo, Noformation, Northernhenge, NorwegianBlue, NotAnonymous0, Notjake13, Nurg, Ohnoitsjamie, Oicumayberight, OlEnglish, Oldlaptop321, Oli Filth, OmnipotentEntity, Opagecrtr, Orphan Wiki, Oxymoron83, PM800, Pandacomics, Panoptical, ParisianBlade, PaulHanson, Pedro, Penbat, Pfuchs722, Pharaoh of the Wizards, Philip Trueman, Philopp, Phobis, Pikiwyn, Pill, Pinar, Pink Bull, Plinkit, Plugwash, Poindexter Propellerhead, Porqin, Possum, Pr sekhar, PrAnAvRoCkS123, Prakashbabugc, Prari, Psantora, Public Menace, Puelof, Pyroglastic, Qistass, Qoforensics, Quaerere, QueenCake, QuiteUnusual, R saji kumar, R4f, RDF, RaminusFalcon, Ranavanita, Rangoon11, Ranveig, Rberkey, Reaperman, Reconsider the static, Reedy, Remi0o, Revo331, RexNL, Reznor34, Rhain1999, Rhobite, Rich Farmbrough, Rjwilmsi, RoRoReRe, Roastytoast, Robbyyy, Roc, Rocastelo, RockMFR, Romaspizza, Ronz, RoonTube, Rrburke, Rror, Rxnd, RyanGerbil10, S04142006, S0IVIE0IVE, SWAdair, Saba qureshi, Sagaci, Saketmitra, Salesvery1, Salvio giuliano, Samgrunners, Sampo, Samsoot, SarekOfVulcan, Satori Son, Scottk, Seaphoto, Sfoskett, Sgw1009, Shab123, Shadowjams, Shawnc, Shaysom09, Shell Kinney, Shravani.pande, Shreshth91, Siva7891, Skizzik, SkyWalker, Slakr, SlayerK, Smithfarm, Smithhogg, So God created Manchester, SoWhy, Sonderbro, Spam kj, Spearhead, Sredojevic96, Sssbbbrrr, Steave77, SteveLoughran, Stonedoc13, Storm Rider, Str3hb, Subhash94666, Suffusion of Yellow, Superbeecat, Superm401, Susahe, Symane, TEB728, Tarun telang, Tbone762, Tedickey, Terry1944, Texture, Thatguyflint, The Anome, The Magnificent Clean-keeper, The Thing That Should Not Be, The Transhumanist (AWB), The undertow, Thedjatclubrock, Thingg, Think outside the box, ThurnerRupert, Tide rolls, Tilmont, Timir2, Tiuks, Tkn20, Tobias Bergemann, Tommy2010, Tony Fox, Tony1, Tpbradbury, Transisto, Traroth, Travelbird, Traxs7, Tregoweth, Trevor MacInnis, Trusilver, Tseno Maximov, Tubeyes, Tuckwell, TwistOfCain, Typhoonchaser, Unique.wiki, UnitedStatesian, Universityalliance, Userafw, Valeria70, Van helsing, Vendeka, Versageek, Vis123, Wackymacs, WaltBusterkeys, Washburnmav, Wavelength, Wendy Scotchmer, Wiki3 1415, WikiLaurent, Wikiborg, Wikipelli, Wimt, Wysprgr2005, Xevious, Xp54321, Yerpo, Yger, Yworo, Zhou Yu, Zidonuke, Zondor, Zsinj, Zzuuzz, 1237 anonymous edits

User_interface *Source*: http://en.wikipedia.org/w/index.php?title=User_interface *Contributors*: Aapo Laitinen, Abelson, Academic Challenger, Acdx, Ageekgal, AlainV, Alanradley, Aleenf1, Alexkon, Alixlouca, Alperkaradas, Amberrock, Andres, Avoided, Baburahwa (chhawni basti), Basawala, Beatmik, Benzbpolo, Betacommand, Bhteam, Bhupendra.meena, Billyg, Billymac00, BioPupil, Bobbyelliott, Boundlessly, Burkhard, CRGreathouse, CSEditor, Call me Bubba, Calltech, Capitocapito, Care2, Casper2k3, Cceli, Chealer, Chris Q, Chrisch, Chun-hian, Clickey, Cometstyles, Crazycomputers, Cuckowski, Curps, D3innovation, DMacks, DXBari, David Haslam, Deguss, DerHexer, Diego Moya, Dragice, Drugonot, Dylan Lake, EagleFan, Edcolins, Effectiveui, Elf-friend, Elmschrat, Epbr123, Erikbrani, Escape Orbit, Espoo, Face, FastLizard4, Fciv, Filemon, Fmccown, Galoubet, GeneMosher, Gepwiki, Ghamer01, Giftlite, Gil Gamesh, Glenn, Haham hanuka, Hariva, Harryboyles, Hdt83, Hede2000, Hetar, Hgamboa, HiDrNick, IIIIIIIII, IceBlade710, Ignorance is strength, Ikescs, Ilovelive1, Imac299, Inductiveautomation, Ios, Isnow, IvanLanin, Ixfd64, Jamelan, Jasper Deng, Jauhienij, Jaxl, Jennycho, Jerryobject, Jgrahn, Jimgawn, KGasso, KJK::Hyperion, Kangham, Kel-nage, Kevin B12, KnightRider, Krushia, Lamalamadingdong, LeaveSleaves, Lee Vonce, Legendsword, Lester, Lightdarkness, Lights, Linkoman, Lkantrov, Lloydpick, LordCirth, Lotje, MCorley, Magioladitis, Majorly, Manop, Marian, MarsRover, Martarius, Mathiastck, Maybury, Merbabu, Merovingian, Michael Hardy, Michael J. Mullany, MichaelMcGuffin, Michal Jurosz, Midgley, MiguelTremblay, Mikael Häggström, Mikrosam Akademija 2, Minghong, Monicahu, Mrh30, Nanshu, Night Gyr, Normxxx, Nurg, Nwbeeson, Owen, Pengo, Pgillman, Philip Trueman, Phydend, Piet Delport, Pigfodder, Piotrus, Plankhead, Pnm, Praba230890, Pwforaker, Pádraic MacUidhir, Qboat, R r245, R'n'B, RMFan1, RYonck, Raven4x4x, Reaperman, RedDragon88, RekishiEJ, Robert Weemeyer, RobertL, Ronz, Roybb95, Rpawson, Ryulong, Sander123, Schastain, Sdmonroe, SebastianHelm, SharksandBears, Shashiraja, Shwetajha671985, Sjakkalle, Slysplace, Smalljim, Spalding, Special Cases, Spinster, Stephenchou0722, SuperColbertFan, TDS, Tamaratrouts, Tasc, Tckma, Tedickey, Telempe, Terra Xin, Texture, The Nut, The Transhumanist, Thelb4, Timir Saxa, Tntdj, Tobias Bergemann, Tony1, Twilightvampirelover, Udo Altmann, Ultraexactzz, Umakant Mishra, Unixguy, Uriash, Veinor, VictorAnyakin, Voidxor, Waggers, Wasami007, Wavelength, Wgoetsch, Whkoh, WikiCantona, WikiLaurent, Willy wonka and the rectum factory, Wrs1864, Wtshymanski, Wysprgr2005, Yannick56, Yashgaroth, Yekrats, Yerpo, Zizzi0n, Санта Клаус, 362 anonymous edits

Software_release_life_cycle *Source*: http://en.wikipedia.org/w/index.php?title=Software_release_life_cycle *Contributors*: -Majestic-, AVRS, Abelson, Aervanath, Aesopos, Ahoerstemeier, Airon90, Ajfd11111, Alansohn, Alereon, Alexander.mitsos, Alexius08, AliveFreeHappy, Amer-aln71, AndrewStellman, Antandrus, Anyanghaseyo, Ariesk47, Ary29, AstareGod, Austro, Azian.otaku, Banazir, Baylink, Ben77, Big-bang1, Black Hornet, BlueDevil, BobHackett, Bobblewik, Bped1985, BruceGrubb, Bubbachuck, Busy Stubber, CH3374H, CapitalSasha, Cherkash, Chris Pickett, Cnilep, Codinghorror, Courcelles, Cpiral, Cprompt, Crazytales, Cybercobra, Cyktsui, Cymru.lass, Daveharr, DavidGrayson, Dcljr, Deb nuke, DemonThing, Denbosch, Derivator, Diagonalfish, Dionyziz, Discospinster, Dlfreem, DmitTrix, DocWatson42, Donbas, Dormant25, Dvdrtrgn, Earthlyreason, Ebear422, Ed g2s, Eet 1024, Eisnel, El Cubano, Electricnet, Ellmist, Elm-39, Epiblitikos, ErkinBatu, Evercat, Evice, Excirial, Eyu100, FaisalJawdat, FatalError, Ferengi, Fiskars007, Flabhead235, FleetCommand, Flowerparty, Frap, Fredrik, Furrykef, Fæ, Gaius Cornelius, Gary Kirk, Giftlite, Gika, GradualStudent, Greg Tyler, Greglo, Grim23, Gyrferret, Hadal, Hede2000, Helge Skjeveland, Helix84, Heyinsun, Hluup, Holek, Homo sapiens, Hotcrocodile, Huttarl, Hvn0413, Hydrogen Iodide, I am Blue 862, IByte, Ice Ardor, Imgaril, IronDiode, Irtaza9993, Itai, JAF1970, JASpencer, Jac16888, JamesGlover, Japo, Jason C.K., JavaTenor, JayC, Jeff G., Jeremy Visser, Jeremyb, Jessemv, Jh51681, Jom, JonHarder, Jorvik, Jsharpminor, Juhachi, Juno12, Kaicarver, Karlthegreat, Katharine908, Kenny Strawn, Kesla, Kjkolb, Knuckles, Krawi, Kwekubo, LOL, Laptopladwiki, Lars Washington, Letdorf, Leuko, Livitup, LizardWizard, Lklundin, Lkopeter, Lolpwnage, Longhair, Lygophile, Lyverbe, M 3bdelqader, M4gnum0n, Mabdul, Mackeriv, Madhero88, Malo, Mark91, Martarius, Martinig, Mateo LeFou, Materialscientist, Mato, Max Naylor, Mcnaugha, Megatyyppi, Mendel, Michael Hardy, Michaelas10, Michig, Mikm, Mindmatrix, Mktos532, Mnemo, Modest Genius, Monty845, Moudrick, MrBlueSky, Mwilso24, NYyankees51, Naryathegreat, Nasir8891, Natzi Boy, Navicular, Nazrila, Nczempin, Neokilly, NeonMerlin, NetRolller 3D, NiceGuyAlberto, NickW557, Nishkid64, Nivix, Noozgroop, Northamerica1000, NuclearWinner, Nurg, Nyp, Octahedron80, OlEnglish, Oni Ookami Alfador, Opensourcejunkie, Padishar, Pallinger, PamD, PanagosTheOther, Paste, Pedant17, Pengo, Petrb, Pgan002, Pgreenspun, Philip Trueman, Pilotguy, Pmsyyz, Po8crg, Pol098, Project2501a, Promethean, Psychosomatic Tumor, Psychotic Spoon, Quest for Truth, Qwerty450, Reaper Eternal, Rehman, Reswobslc, Rgb9000, Rich Farmbrough, Riffraffselbow, Riumplus, Rj, Rjwilmsi, Robert K S, Robinson James, Romanc19s, Ronark, Ronhjones, RoySmith, Schapel, Sd31415, Seaphoto, Shadowjams, Shepard, Singularity, Sitearm, Skeejay, Sleske, Someone else, Sparkyguy10, Spasemunki, Spliffy, Srikant.sharma, StuieT, Swfblade, SwisterTwister, Swwright, Sykopomp, TakuyaMurata, Tatatstr, Technobadger, Thatdog, The Thing That Should Not Be, TheTallOne, Thedivinehacker, Thegreenj, Thesquire, Thumperward, Tiddly Tom, Tom Matteinen, Tomasf, Tomchen1989, Tommy2010, Topher385,

Totalirrelevance, Towel401, Travelbird, Tverbeek, Ukexpat, Unyoyega, ViperSnake151, Vmadeira, WalterGR, Warren, Wavelength, Wayiran, Wdd123, Whatkindofausernameisthis, Whoisjohngalt, Wiki Jazz man, Wikibofh, Wikibrent, Wwwwolf, X-Fi6, XJamRastafire, Yoshiisgod, Zacatecnik, Zarel, Zeimusu, Zero10one, ZeroOne, Zerofire0, Zundark, 594 anonymous edits

Independent_film *Source*: http://en.wikipedia.org/w/index.php?title=Independent_film *Contributors*: *drew, 220 of Borg, 7of7equals0, 8mmfilm!, Abtinb, Acka jacka, Addinfo43, Ahmet1977, Al Fecund, Alex morris is cool, AlexTheMartian, Alexbonaro, Algae, AlistairMcMillan, Aliyah.jmohammed, Analoguedragon, Anetode, Animated Cascade, Anoopkn, Araiderplaya, Asasa64, Ash1028, Asstjeff, AudioHawk, BICHOLUCA, Barnhartjr, Bbarringer, Beetstra, Bert bert, Biffwinters, Big Bird, Bjdehut, Blah, blah, blah, Bluebird29, Bobblewik, Bobo The Ninja, BooZker, Calgary, Camerado, CanadianLinuxUser, Cantina.band, Casey14, Ccfilms, Ceoil, Cfsenel, Chhowe, Cigarette, Cindery, Cinmea14, Ckatz, ClementSeveillac, CodeMonk, Cop 663, Cornellrockey, Custardninja, D6, DVD R W, Dan aka jack, DavidMcClurg, Davinhutchins, Davmpls, Deglr6328, Dictatormovie, Digital-ent, Discospinster, Dougweller, Duncancumming, Dutzi, EmeraldB, Empoor, Everyking, FMAFan1990, Falcan61, Falcon in air, Fan-1967, Febrero, FelixNawothnig, Fergaliscious, FilmCalls, Filmmakingstuff, Filmsharing, Filmuser99, Firsfron, Floboskifilms, Foobaz, Frap, FredR, Freshh, FrostyBytes, Futileboy, G4COM, Gaius Cornelius, Gakusha, GamblinMonkey, Gerrit, Giancarlo Rossi, Giraffedata, Gmoose1, GoingBatty, Golbez, GreyCat, Grosscha, Ground Zero, Guillom, Guy Harris, H, HannoverHouse, Hans Dunkelberg, Hawkhkg11, Hellosandimas, Herostratus, HisSpaceResearch, Hiwhispees, Hoseumou, Hu12, HuguesdeSaintSalvy, Hut 8.5, ILovePlankton, Iamhuman2010, Ianisarebl, Ianweller, Ielsner, Imroy, In Defense of the Artist, Ina-178, Indie Film, Inkykopp, Iraethan, Iridescent, Irishguy, J.delanoy, J36miles, JRobertB2, Jackp, Jagged 85, Jahsonic, Jamesarthurconrad, Jay-W, JayDez, Jayron32, Jeff G., Jerry Anderson, Jevansen, Jguerrero15, Jivemantz, John Carter, John of Reading, Johncmorley, Jon Harald Søby, JordoCo, Josh Parris, Journalist, Jtalledo, Julie18282, Junkpalace, Jus1haz2, KCS de RBM, Katie Button, Kbh3rd, Kf4bdy, Khym Chanur, Kman2025, Koavf, Krasimir, Kufu91, Kushboy, Kyorosuke, Labanex, Lakers, LeCire, Leonardo2505, LeyteWolfer, Lilac Soul, Lockley, Logicwillbreak.yourheart, M1angr42, MCW07, MadAve, MadHitcher, Manticore, Martarius, Marychan41, Marye574, Mats Helge, Max Terry, Mccready, Mdwh, Melaniesharrison, Merkelbachfilms, Mertallix, Metropolitan90, Mfk91, Mfu254, Michael Hardy, MichaelJanich, MichaelMoore, Mike902, MikeWazowski, Mikus, Milkbartoilet, Mindmatrix, Mintleaf, Mitsukai, Mlaffs, Morda898, Mr 1234, Mrs. Wolpoff, Mrwuggs, Mushroom, Musicman42991, Nadesai, Nate Speed, Navanil, Nayenflies, Nickgiant, Nickptar, Nigholith, Nikko11, Nneonneo, Ogat, Omananda, OnBeyondZebrax, Onejaguar, Oxygarum, PC78, Packing, Patrick, Pernelldh, Photoactivist, PiedPiper, Pigman, Pipistrello2004, Prayer for the wild at heart, Preslethe, Pteranodon, Qutezuce, RadicalBender, RepublicanJacobite, Researchindie, Rhoody, Rich Farmbrough, RiverRubicon, Rjwilmsi, Rkb669, Runa27, Russ47025, Ryanasaurus0077, Saber girl08, Sabrebd, Saganaki-, Salam32, Sasuke Sarutobi, Savionlife, Scales, Seba5618, Sektor0514, Serein (renamed because of SUL), Shawn in Montreal, Shirulashem, Shoetoeeater, SiobhanHansa, Skier Dude, Skomorokh, Smofficeman, Sniperzgonewild, Soriano329, Soumyasch, Sssoul, Steel, Student Learner 101, Sullenspice, Surfdarthvader, Sxeptomaniac, TFNorman, TKD, TMC1221, TamsinW, Tbmreditor, Thaman81, Thatbadwoman, The MARVEL, The Wookieepedian, TheChrisD, TheRealFennShysa, Theamazingspiderman20, Themfromspace, Thomas Larsen, Tide rolls, Tmacin, Tsemii, Tvpixelvision, Twinsday, Uncle G, UncleDunkel, Unopeneddoor, Vanscott31, Vipersquad, Wadegasque, Weiyanhua2005, Whoville, WikiTome, Wikipedia brown, William.Weatherington, Wimt, Wisco, Woahdolla, Wolfling, Xblack13, Yamazon3, ZacharyColbert1, Zondor, A, נאונלוק', , 638 anonymous edits

Sundance_Film_Festival *Source*: http://en.wikipedia.org/w/index.php?title=Sundance_Film_Festival *Contributors*: 2sc945, 66.74.87.xxx, 72Dino, A, A7K, Abdallahdjabi, Agent 86, Alan smithee, AlexLevyOne, Amoammo, Annexia, Arpingstone, Ash, B.arjun, BD2412, Bdorfman, Bearcat, Before My Ken, Belovedfreak, Ben-Zin, Bevo, Binderhead, Blessing-light, Bobblewik, BostonRed, CDaly, Cathygiffi, ChrisBrown, ChrisKil, Chriso852, Ckatz, Clemmy, ColdCase, Conversion script, Coralmizu, Courcelles, Crunch, Cryan71, Cubs Fan, Custardninja, Dasani, DaviddesJ, Dezidor, Diafygi, Donteatyellowsnow, Dravecky, Dwoodwoo, Earlypsychosis, Eastdakota, Eipnvn, Emperorbma, Encycloshave, Entheta, Erianna, Etiquette05, Evil Monkey, Famspear, Fatal exception, Feather Jonah, Femto, Filmerbob, Frecklefoot, Freshairr, Goodmachiners, Graham87, Greks224, Gurch, HJ Mitchell, Hadal, HappyDog, Harry Cassidy, Harry3221, Hbent, Hoverfish, Hoyhoy311, Hubertfarnsworth, Hypermagic, IdanE, JGKlein, JSmith60, Jabbasi, Jack Merridew, JahmezL, Janus303, Jatkins, Jeffwilser, Jennyselby, Jester2001, Jllm06, JoanneB, John, Johndbeatty, JonMoore, Jonathan.s.kt, Jonwillig, JustAGal, Justme89, Kafziel, Kariteh, Ke5crz, Kent Wang, Ketiltrout, Kevinthompson3221, Kodster, Kollision, Krukouski, Lashaneria, Lflint165, LilHelpa, Logan, Malepheasant, MarkGyver, Markhakd, Martarius, Martin451, Maximoff77, Momentarydogma, Mosmof, Mrjamin, NameIsRon, Nicke Lilltroll, Nihonjoe, Nohat, Noted Seven, Octopod, OnBeyondZebrax, Ospinad, Otto4711, P2455, Pangloss, Pdfpdf, Pearle, Phil Boswell, Pilar.morgan, Postdlf, Ppntori, Puckly, Qaqaq, Quatloo, R'n'B, Reginmund, Rich Farmbrough, Rich jj, Rick Block, Rje, Rjwilmsi, RlyehRising, Rmky87, RossPatterson, Rray, Runa27, Screamfestla, Sephiroth BCR, Sepia tone, Shizhao, Sleepyjuly, Snoyes, SomebodysDad, SpikeJones, Stonnman, Strawberryfire, Superoxen, SusanLesch, Szalas, T3hmyth, TCGlibrary, TKD, Tbhotch, Th1rt3en, The Crevasse, TheLeopard, Thedarknight666, Torkmann, Tubafatness, USAFF, Ulric1313, Uncle Dick, Vina, Wars, Wildtornado, Wisekwai, Wolfpackfan72, Xandi, Youssefsan, Zeno Gantner, Ziel, A, 247 anonymous edits

Bad_Robot_Productions *Source*: http://en.wikipedia.org/w/index.php?title=Bad_Robot_Productions *Contributors*: Aatrek, AdamDeanHall, Admaiore, Ajhoax, Albert109, Alex IW12, Analogue Kid, Andrewericoleman, Antiadmn, Arichnad, ArkansasTraveler, Azumanga1, Batman tas, Bearcat, Bencey, BookDen, BurgerKingFanatic, CLW, Cbmanley, Chris the speller, Chrisplyon, Crjeong, CultureDrone, Deconstructhis, Deli nk, Don-Don, Dputig07, EWikist, Empoor, Farpointer, Faster2010, FrankRizzo2006, Hippopotamus, HollywoodAllstars, Imagine Reason, J. Fanning, John, John of Reading, Josiah Rowe, Jtalledo, JustAGal, K1Bond007, Kellogg257, Kwedin, Leaf2001br, Lemonium, LiamNolan15212, Mark Jensen, Martarius, Merci, Mithos90, Modeset, Mrceleb2007, Mtjaws, My Cat inn, NGMan62, No14mike, Noclevername, Nwh5305, Oldag07, Pascal.Tesson, Pegship, Physicistjedi, PrisonMan, Pwojdacz, Qwyrxian, RadicalBender, Richard Arthur Norton (1958-), Rilonator666, Robsinden, Roger McCoy, Rusted AutoParts, SD6-Agent, Salocin, Shinmawa, SimonP, SkeletorUK, Snowblink, Sobnambulist, Socby19, Squeck, Stuartmarsh913, Swerdnaneb, TDogg310, Tassedethe, TenPoundHammer, TerokNor, The JPS, The wub, TheLastAmigo, TheRealFennShysa, TheValentineBros, Theda, ThomasSixten, ThylekShran, Tracer9999, Trivialist, TubularWorld, Ty.tremblay, Typhoon966, Warpozio, Wikimanage77, Woohookitty, X!, Yashx0x, 241 anonymous edits

Spyglass_Entertainment *Source*: http://en.wikipedia.org/w/index.php?title=Spyglass_Entertainment *Contributors*: AdamDeanHall, Adrian 1001, AniMate, Anonymous101, Arx Fortis, Bbb23, BenPhil, Bencey, Bigkhrisdogg, Bilbo571, Biyos, Bull-Doser, CWenger, CambridgeBayWeather, Cayla, Clickophone Guy, CoolKatt number 99999, CoolMatt444, Cooliocheck1, CraigFoye80, DKqwerty, DocWatson42, Don-Don, Drpickem, Erik, Escape Orbit, FMAFan1990, Flowerpotman, FrankRizzo2006, Freshh, GCL, Gogo Dodo, Gr1st, Graham87, Grandpafootsoldier, Gwernol, Holladio, J. Fanning, J.delanoy, Jean.julius, Jedi94, Jevon Tompkins, Jfromrepublica, JohnnyL80, JonathanKao23, Jpoulin123456789, Jwein, Keppa, Kieranthompson, Klltr, Kusunose, Kyle van der Meer, Lemonium, Lotje, Majorclanger, Martarius, MasashiInoue, McCloud-Mallowolf, McDoobAU93, MikeAllen, MikeWazowski, Mynameisjerrymreh, Noclador, OllieFury, Pascal.Tesson, PatrikR, Pennyinkwell, Prolog, R craycroft, RA0808, RicJac, Rich257, Roachie, Ryanasaurus007, Ryulong, ShelfSkewed, Shenme, Shortride, Sjones23, Squids and Chips, Steve, SummerPhD, T, TMC1982, Tassedethe, Taylor Karras, Tbhotch, The GateKeeper07, The Movie King!, The Rogue Penguin, The wub, TheRealFennShysa, TheValentineBros, Thorwald, ThylekShran, Tinlinkin, TracyLinkEdnaVelmaPenny, Tregoweth, Trogga, Typhoon966, Urbanrenewal, Vusys, Wakumon2000, Ward3001, WebbyTaranula44444, Wiki alf, ZrzlKing, 617 anonymous edits

Image Sources, Licenses and Contributors

File:Android 4.0.png *Source*: http://en.wikipedia.org/w/index.php?title=File:Android_4.0.png *License*: unknown *Contributors*: Android Open Source project

Image:2005ICT.PNG *Source*: http://en.wikipedia.org/w/index.php?title=File:2005ICT.PNG *License*: unknown *Contributors*: Mdd, Shushruth, 1 anonymous edits

File:00-bma-automation-operator-panel-with-pushbuttons.JPG *Source*: http://en.wikipedia.org/w/index.php?title=File:00-bma-automation-operator-panel-with-pushbuttons.JPG *License*: unknown *Contributors*: User:Elmschrat

File:Software dev2.svg *Source*: http://en.wikipedia.org/w/index.php?title=File:Software_dev2.svg *License*: unknown *Contributors*: User:Heyinsun

File:Sundance-Film-Festival.jpg *Source*: http://en.wikipedia.org/w/index.php?title=File:Sundance-Film-Festival.jpg *License*: unknown *Contributors*: Bawolff, Kilom691, Nikita

Image:BadRobotLOGONEW.jpg *Source*: http://en.wikipedia.org/w/index.php?title=File:BadRobotLOGONEW.jpg *License*: unknown *Contributors*: Chrisplyon, Melesse, Pwojdacz

Image:Bad Robot Productions logo.jpg *Source*: http://en.wikipedia.org/w/index.php?title=File:Bad_Robot_Productions_logo.jpg *License*: unknown *Contributors*: User:Pwojdacz

Image:Spyglass Entertainment.jpg *Source*: http://en.wikipedia.org/w/index.php?title=File:Spyglass_Entertainment.jpg *License*: unknown *Contributors*: Calmer Waters, Grandpafootsoldier

GNU Free Documentation License Version 1.2, November 2002 Copyright (C) 2000,2001,2002 Free Software Foundation, Inc. 59 Temple Place, Suite 330, Boston, MA 02111-1307 USA Everyone is permitted to copy and distribute verbatim copies of this license document, but changing it is not allowed.

0. PREAMBLE

The purpose of this License is to make a manual, textbook, or other functional and useful document "free" in the sense of freedom: to assure everyone the effective freedom to copy and redistribute it, with or without modifying it, either commercially or noncommercially. Secondarily, this License preserves for the author and publisher a way to get credit for their work, while not being considered responsible for modifications made by others. This License is a kind of "copyleft", which means that derivative works of the document must themselves be free in the same sense. It complements the GNU General Public License, which is a copyleft license designed for free software. We have designed this License in order to use it for manuals for free software, because free software needs free documentation: a free program should come with manuals providing the same freedoms that the software does. But this License is not limited to software manuals; it can be used for any textual work, regardless of subject matter or whether it is published as a printed book. We recommend this License principally for works whose purpose is instruction or reference.

1. APPLICABILITY AND DEFINITIONS

This License applies to any manual or other work, in any medium, that contains a notice placed by the copyright holder saying it can be distributed under the terms of this License. Such a notice grants a world-wide, royalty-free license, unlimited in duration, to use that work under the conditions stated herein. The "Document", below, refers to any such manual or work. Any member of the public is a licensee, and is addressed as "you". You accept the license if you copy, modify or distribute the work in a way requiring permission under copyright law. A "Modified Version" of the Document means any work containing the Document or a portion of it, either copied verbatim, or with modifications and/or translated into another language. A "Secondary Section" is a named appendix or a front-matter section of the Document that deals exclusively with the relationship of the publishers or authors of the Document to the Document's overall subject (or to related matters) and contains nothing that could fall directly within that overall subject. (Thus, if the Document is in part a textbook of mathematics, a Secondary Section may not explain any mathematics.) The relationship could be a matter of historical connection with the subject or with related matters, or of legal, commercial, philosophical, ethical or political position regarding them. The "Invariant Sections" are certain Secondary Sections whose titles are designated, as being those of Invariant Sections, in the notice that says that the Document is released under this License. If a section does not fit the above definition of Secondary then it is not allowed to be designated as Invariant. The Document may contain zero Invariant Sections. If the Document does not identify any Invariant Sections then there are none. The "Cover Texts" are certain short passages of text that are listed, as Front-Cover Texts or Back-Cover Texts, in the notice that says that the Document is released under this License. A Front-Cover Text may be at most 5 words, and a Back-Cover Text may be at most 25 words. A "Transparent" copy of the Document means a machine-readable copy, represented in a format whose specification is available to the general public, that is suitable for revising the document straightforwardly with generic text editors or (for images composed of pixels) generic paint programs or (for drawings) some widely available drawing editor, and that is suitable for input to text formatters or for automatic translation to a variety of formats suitable for input to text formatters. A copy made in an otherwise Transparent file format whose markup, or absence of markup, has been arranged to thwart or discourage subsequent modification by readers is not Transparent. An image format is not Transparent if used for any substantial amount of text. A copy that is not "Transparent" is called "Opaque". Examples of suitable formats for Transparent copies include plain ASCII without markup, Texinfo input format, LaTeX input format, SGML or XML using a publicly available DTD, and standard-conforming simple HTML, PostScript or PDF designed for human modification. Examples of transparent image formats include PNG, XCF and JPG. Opaque formats include proprietary formats that can be read and edited only by proprietary word processors, SGML or XML for which the DTD and/or processing tools are not generally available, and the machine-generated HTML, PostScript or PDF produced by some word processors for output purposes only. The "Title Page" means, for a printed book, the title page itself, plus such following pages as are needed to hold, legibly, the material this License requires to appear in the title page. For works in formats which do not have any title page as such, "Title Page" means the text near the most prominent appearance of the work's title, preceding the beginning of the body of the text. A section "Entitled XYZ" means a named subunit of the Document whose title either is precisely XYZ or contains XYZ in parentheses following text that translates XYZ in another language. (Here XYZ stands for a specific section name mentioned below, such as "Acknowledgements", "Dedications", "Endorsements", or "History".) To "Preserve the Title" of such a section when you modify the Document means that it remains a section "Entitled XYZ" according to this definition. The Document may include Warranty Disclaimers next to the notice which states that this License applies to the Document. These Warranty Disclaimers are considered to be included by reference in this License, but only as regards disclaiming warranties: any other implication that these Warranty Disclaimers may have is void and has no effect on the meaning of this License.

2. VERBATIM COPYING

You may copy and distribute the Document in any medium, either commercially or noncommercially, provided that this License, the copyright notices, and the license notice saying this License applies to the Document are reproduced in all copies, and that you add no other conditions whatsoever to those of this License. You may not use technical measures to obstruct or control the reading or further copying of the copies you make or distribute. However, you may accept compensation in exchange for copies. If you distribute a large enough number of copies you must also follow the conditions in section 3. You may also lend copies, under the same conditions stated above, and you may publicly display copies.

3. COPYING IN QUANTITY

If you publish printed copies (or copies in media that commonly have printed covers) of the Document, numbering more than 100, and the Document's license notice requires Cover Texts, you must enclose the copies in covers that carry, clearly and legibly, all these Cover Texts: Front-Cover Texts on the front cover, and Back-Cover Texts on the back cover. Both covers must also clearly and legibly identify you as the publisher of these copies. The front cover must present the full title with all words of the title equally prominent and visible. You may add other material on the covers in addition. Copying with changes limited to the covers, as long as they preserve the title of the Document and satisfy these conditions, can be treated as verbatim copying in other respects. If the required texts for either cover are too voluminous to fit legibly, you should put the first ones listed (as many as fit reasonably) on the actual cover, and continue the rest onto adjacent pages. If you publish or distribute Opaque copies of the Document numbering more than 100, you must either include a machine-readable Transparent copy along with each Opaque copy, or state in or with each Opaque copy a computer-network location from which the general network-using public has access to download using public-standard network protocols a complete Transparent copy of the Document, free of added material. If you use the latter option, you must take reasonably prudent steps, when you begin distribution of Opaque copies in quantity, to ensure that this Transparent copy will remain thus accessible at the stated location until at least one year after the last time you distribute an Opaque copy (directly or through your agents or retailers) of that edition to the public. It is requested, but not required, that you contact the authors of the Document well before redistributing any large number of copies, to give them a chance to provide you with an updated version of the Document.

4. MODIFICATIONS

You may copy and distribute a Modified Version of the Document under the conditions of sections 2 and 3 above, provided that you release the Modified Version under precisely this License, with the Modified Version filling the role of the Document, thus licensing distribution and modification of the Modified Version to whoever possesses a copy of it. In addition, you must do these things in the Modified Version: A. Use in the Title Page (and on the covers, if any) a title distinct from that of the Document, and from those of previous versions (which should, if there were any, be listed in the History section of the Document). You may use the same title as a previous version if the original publisher of that version gives permission. B. List on the Title Page, as authors, one or more persons or entities responsible for authorship of the modifications in the Modified Version, together with at least five of the principal authors of the Document (all of its principal authors, if it has fewer than five), unless they release you from this requirement. C. State on the Title page the name of the publisher of the Modified Version, as the publisher. D. Preserve all the copyright notices of the Document. E. Add an appropriate copyright notice for your modifications adjacent to the other copyright notices. F. Include, immediately after the copyright notices, a license notice giving the public permission to use the Modified Version under the terms of this License, in the form shown in the Addendum below. G. Preserve in that license notice the full lists of Invariant Sections and required Cover Texts given in the Document's license notice. H. Include an unaltered copy of this License. I. Preserve the section Entitled "History", Preserve its Title, and add to it an item stating at least the title, year, new authors, and publisher of the Modified Version as given on the Title Page. If there is no section Entitled "History" in the Document, create one stating the title, year, authors, and publisher of the Document as given on its Title Page, then add an item describing the Modified Version as stated in the previous sentence. J. Preserve the network location, if any, given in the Document for public access to a Transparent copy of the Document, and likewise the network locations given in the Document for previous versions it was based on. These may be placed in the "History" section. You may omit a network location for a work that was published at least four years before the Document itself, or if the original publisher of the version it refers to gives permission. K. For any section Entitled "Acknowledgements" or "Dedications", Preserve the Title of the section, and preserve in the section all the substance and tone of each of the contributor acknowledgements and/or dedications given therein. L. Preserve all the Invariant Sections of the Document, unaltered in their text and in their titles. Section numbers or the equivalent are not considered part of the section titles. M. Delete any section Entitled "Endorsements". Such a section may not be included in the Modified Version. N. Do not retitle any existing section to be Entitled "Endorsements" or to conflict in title with any Invariant Section. O. Preserve any Warranty Disclaimers. If the Modified Version includes new front-matter sections or appendices that qualify as Secondary Sections and contain no material copied from the Document, you may at your option designate some or all of these sections as invariant. To do this, add their titles to the list of Invariant Sections in the Modified Version's license notice. These titles must be distinct from any other section titles. You may add a section Entitled "Endorsements", provided it contains nothing but endorsements of your Modified Version by various parties--for example, statements of peer review or that the text has been approved by an organization as the authoritative definition of a standard. You may add a passage of up to five words as a Front-Cover Text, and a passage of up to 25 words as a Back-Cover Text, to the end of the list of Cover Texts in the Modified Version. Only one passage of Front-Cover Text and one of Back-Cover Text may be added by (or through arrangements made by) any one entity. If the Document already includes a cover text for the same cover, previously added by you or by arrangement made by the same entity you are acting on behalf of, you may not add another; but you may replace the old one, on explicit permission from the previous publisher that added the old one. The author(s) and publisher(s) of the Document do not by this License give permission to use their names for publicity for or to assert or imply endorsement of any Modified Version.

5. COMBINING DOCUMENTS

You may combine the Document with other documents released under this License, under the terms defined in section 4 above for modified versions, provided that you include in the combination all of the Invariant Sections of all of the original documents, unmodified, and list them all as Invariant Sections of your combined work in its license notice, and that you preserve all their Warranty Disclaimers. The combined work need only contain one copy of this License, and multiple identical Invariant Sections may be replaced with a single copy. If there are multiple Invariant Sections with the same name but different contents, make the title of each such section unique by adding at the end of it, in parentheses, the name of the original author or publisher of that section if known, or else a unique number. Make the same adjustment to the section titles in the list of Invariant Sections in the license notice of the combined work. In the combination, you must combine any sections Entitled "History" in the various original documents, forming one section Entitled "History"; likewise combine any sections Entitled "Acknowledgements", and any sections Entitled "Dedications". You must delete all sections Entitled "Endorsements".

6. COLLECTIONS OF DOCUMENTS

You may make a collection consisting of the Document and other documents released under this License, and replace the individual copies of this License in the various documents with a single copy that is included in the collection, provided that you follow the rules of this License for verbatim copying of each of the documents in all other respects. You may extract a single document from such a collection, and distribute it individually under this License, provided you insert a copy of this License into the extracted document, and follow this License in all other respects regarding verbatim copying of that document.

7. AGGREGATION WITH INDEPENDENT WORKS

A compilation of the Document or its derivatives with other separate and independent documents or works, in or on a volume of a storage or distribution medium, is called an "aggregate" if the copyright resulting from the compilation is not used to limit the legal rights of the compilation's users beyond what the individual works permit. When the Document is included in an aggregate, this License does not apply to the other works in the aggregate which are not themselves derivative works of the Document. If the Cover Text requirement of section 3 is applicable to these copies of the Document, then if the Document is less than one half of the entire aggregate, the Document's Cover Texts may be placed on covers that bracket the Document within the aggregate, or the electronic equivalent of covers if the Document is in electronic form. Otherwise they must appear on printed covers that bracket the whole aggregate.

8. TRANSLATION

Translation is considered a kind of modification, so you may distribute translations of the Document under the terms of section 4. Replacing Invariant Sections with translations requires special permission from their copyright holders, but you may include translations of some or all Invariant Sections in addition to the original versions of these Invariant Sections. You may include a translation of this License, and all the license notices in the Document, and any Warranty Disclaimers, provided that you also include the original English version of this License and the original versions of those notices and disclaimers. In case of a disagreement between the translation and the original version of this License or a notice or disclaimer, the original version will prevail. If a section in the Document is Entitled "Acknowledgements", "Dedications", or "History", the requirement (section 4) to Preserve its Title (section 1) will typically require changing the actual title.

9. TERMINATION

You may not copy, modify, sublicense, or distribute the Document except as expressly provided for under this License. Any other attempt to copy, modify, sublicense or distribute the Document is void, and will automatically terminate your rights under this License. However, parties who have received copies, or rights, from you under this License will not have their licenses terminated so long as such parties remain in full compliance.

10. FUTURE REVISIONS OF THIS LICENSE

The Free Software Foundation may publish new, revised versions of the GNU Free Documentation License from time to time. Such new versions will be similar in spirit to the present version, but may differ in detail to address new problems or concerns. See http://www.gnu.org/copyleft/. Each version of the License is given a distinguishing version number. If the Document specifies that a particular numbered version of this License "or any later version" applies to it, you have the option of following the terms and conditions either of that specified version or of any later version that has been published (not as a draft) by the Free Software Foundation. If the Document does not specify a version number of this License, you may choose any version ever published (not as a draft) by the Free Software Foundation. ADDENDUM: How to use this License for your documents To use this License in a document you have written, include a copy of the License in the document and put the following copyright and license notices just after the title page: Copyright (c) YEAR YOUR NAME. Permission is granted to copy, distribute and/or modify this document under the terms of the GNU Free Documentation License, Version 1.2 or any later version published by the Free Software Foundation; with no Invariant Sections, no Front-Cover Texts, and no Back-Cover Texts. A copy of the license is included in the section entitled "GNU Free Documentation License". If you have Invariant Sections, Front-Cover Texts and Back-Cover Texts, replace the "with...Texts." line with this: with the Invariant Sections being LIST THEIR TITLES, with the Front-Cover Texts being LIST, and with the Back-Cover Texts being LIST. If you have Invariant Sections without Cover Texts, or some other combination of the three, merge those two alternatives to suit the situation. If your document contains nontrivial examples of program code, we recommend releasing these examples in parallel under your choice of free software license, such as the GNU General Public License, to permit their use in free software.

Printed by Books on Demand GmbH, Norderstedt / Germany